Longman
PHOTO DICTIONARY
Beginning Workbook

Marjorie Fuchs

Longman Photo Dictionary Beginning Workbook

Longman Inc., 95 Church Street, White Plains, N.Y. 10601

Associated companies:
Longman Group Ltd., London
Longman Cheshire Pty., Melbourne
Longman Paul Pty., Auckland
Copp Clark Pitman, Toronto
Pitman Publishing Inc., New York

Distributed in the United Kingdom by Longman Group Ltd., Longman House, Burnt Hill, Harlow, Essex CM20 2JE, England, and by associated companies, branches and representatives throughout the world.

Executive editor: Joanne Dresner
Development editor: Karen Davy
Production editor: Helen B. Ambrosio
Text & cover design: Joseph DePinho
Cover photo: John Edelman
Text art: Joseph DePinho, Susan J. Moore , Jill Francis Wood
Production supervisor: Helen B. Ambrosio

ISBN 0-8013-0249-8

88 89 90 91 92 93 9 8 7 6 5 4 3 2 1

CONTENTS

1 NUMBERS · TIME

1 Match the words in column A with the numbers and symbols in column B.

	A		B
1. _d_	two		a. 11
2. _c_	eighteen		b. 3/4
3. _b_	three quarters		c. 31
4. _h_	eighty		d. 2
5. _j_	one third		e. 80
6. _c_	thirty-one		f. ×
7. _g_	equals		g. =
8. _f_	times		h. 18
9. _11_	eleven		i. 80,000
10. _i_	eighty thousand		j. 1/3

2 Listen and write the numbers.

1. My address is __25__ East __4th__ th Street.

2. My zip code is __17649__

3. My phone number is __5839924__ .

4. My area code is __719__ .

5. My social security number is __128489823__.

3 Complete the charts.

	_____
	(your name)
address	_____
zip code	_____
phone	(___) _____

	_____
	(friend's name)
address	_____
zip code	_____
phone	(___) _____

4 Correct the math test.

Put an X next to the wrong answers.

Give the test a grade (each correct question = 10%).

Math

X 1. 4 + 6 = **9**   6. 31 + 72 = **103**

2. 4 ÷ 4 = **1**   7. 88 ÷ 4 = **22**

3. 3 × 3 = **9**   8. 19 × 5 = **105**

4. 18 − 7 = **12**   9. 248 ÷ 2 = **124**

5. 70 − 13 = **57**   10. 300 − 50 = **250**

Number one is wrong. Four plus six is ten.

2

5 Read the sentences.

Decide who lives in the first, second, third, and fourth apartments.

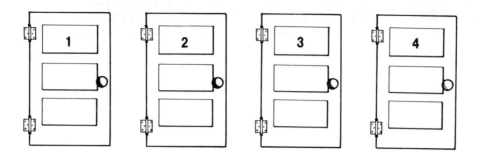

Vilma doesn't live in the fourth apartment.
Bill lives between Vilma and Cathy.
Vilma lives between Bill and Tom.
Tom doesn't live in the first apartment.

1. Vilma lives in the _____ apartment.

2. Cathy _____ .

3. Bill _____ .

4. Tom _____ .

6 Cross out the time that is different.

1. three thirty   half past three   three thirteen

2. five ten   ten to five   five after ten

3. seven forty   twenty to eight   seven to four

4. eight o'clock   eight thirty   eight

5. midnight   twelve o'clock   two o'clock

6. one P.M.   one in the morning   one in the afternoon

3

2 CALENDAR & HOLIDAYS WEATHER & SEASONS

1 Unscramble the names of the months.
Put them in the correct order.

____ uejn _____   ____ pairl _____

____ carmh _____   ____ btoocer _____

____ amy _____   ____ tugaus _____

____ moenbrve _____   _1_ aryjuna *January*

____ buyferar _____   ____ rcembeed _____

____ etespembr _____   ____ yujl _____

2 Read the sentences and write <u>True</u> or <u>False</u>.
Correct the sentences that are false.

1. Easter is in <u>August</u>.

   False. Easter is in April.

2. There are <u>two holidays</u> in March.

   _____

3. Mother's Day and Father's Day are in <u>May</u>.

   _____

4. There are <u>no</u> holidays in August.

   _____

4

3 **Look at the thermometers.**

Complete the sentences with a word from the box.

below freezing	freezing
cold	h̶o̶t̶
cool	warm

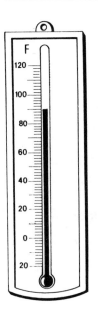 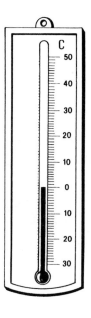 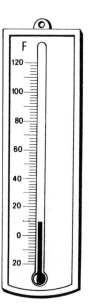

1. It's *hot* . 2. It's _____ . 3. It's _____ .

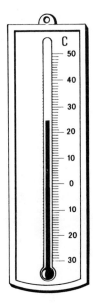 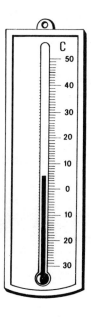

4. It's _____ . 5. It's _____ . 6. It's _____ .

4 Cross out the word that does not belong.

1. Monday   Thursday   ~~January~~   Friday

2. Labor Day   Sunday   Father's Day   Christmas

3. summer   sunny   winter   fall

4. cold   hot   chilly   windy

5. March   Monday   October   July

6. sunny   stormy   spring   snowy

5 Listen to the weather forecast and circle the word you hear.

Here's the _____ forecast for tomorrow, _____
         1. winter / (weather)   2. (January) / February

fifth. Tomorrow will be _____ and _____ in the morning
               3. (sunny) / stormy   4. rainy / (windy)

with temperatures around _____ . _____ will also be
                5. (freezing) / fifteen 6. Tuesday / (Thursday)

very _____ , the temperature dropping to below _____ .
   7. cool / (cold)   8. (fifteen) / freezing

6 Answer the questions.

1. When is your birthday?

_____

2. What days do you have English class?

_____

3. How is the weather today?

_____

4. What is the temperature?

_____

3 SHAPES & MEASUREMENTS

1 Match the pictures in column A with the words in column B.

	A	**B**
1. *d*		a. oval
2. ___	(oval)	b. circle
3. ___	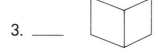	c. triangle
4. ___	(triangle)	d. square
5. ___	(cylinder)	e. cube
6. ___	(circle)	f. cylinder

2 A man wants to buy some curtains.
Listen and circle the word you hear.

MAN: I'd like to buy some curtains.

SALESPERSON: Fine. Do you have the _____?
                    1. meters / (measurements)

MAN: Yes. The _____ is 10 _____, and the
                    2. (length) / width   3. (feet) / meters

_____ is _____ feet.
4. length / (width)   5. (4) / 5

3   **Read the sentences.**

Look at the pictures and write True or False.

Correct the sentences that are false.

1. This is a circle.

False. It's a spiral.

2. Line A is parallel to line B.

_____

3. This is an isosceles triangle.

_____

4. The width of this rectangle is 8 inches.

_____

5. Line X is the diagonal.

_____

6. The X is on the front of the cube.

_____

4 Study the picture.

Cover it with a piece of paper.

Read the words in the box and put a check (√) next to the shapes in the picture.

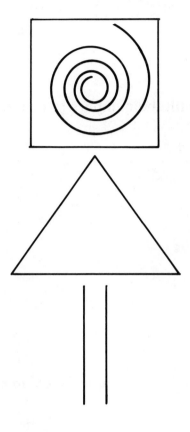

oval	square
√ triangle	parallel lines
radius	perpendicular lines
rectangle	circle
spiral	cylinder

4 MONEY & BANKING

1 Match the words in column A with the numbers in column B.

	A		B
1. _c_	dime	a.	$10.00
2. ___	quarter	b.	1¢
3. ___	penny	c.	10¢
4. ___	nickel	d.	25¢
5. ___	ten dollars	e.	5¢

2 Match the words in column A with the pictures in column B.

A   B

1. _d_ quarter   a.

2. ___ half dollar   b.

3. ___ twenty dollars   c.

4. ___ silver dollar   d.

5. ___ fifteen dollars   e.

3 Complete the checks with the missing numbers.

1.

Richard M. Smith

Dec. 1 19 _90_

Pay to the Order of _Daphne Edwards_ | $ _29.00_

Twenty-nine and ××/100 ___ Dollars

MADISON SAVINGS BANK

For_____ _Richard M. Smith_

2.

Norma Green

Dec. 1 19 _90_

Pay to the Order of _Dr. Lee_ | $ _50.00_

and ××/100 Dollars

MADISON SAVINGS BANK

For_____ _Norma Green_

3.

Joseph Lopey

Dec. 1 19 _90_

Pay to the Order of _Texas Electric Co._ | $ [ ]

Fourteen and ××/100 ___ Dollars

MADISON SAVINGS BANK

For_____ _Joseph Lopey_

4.

Wanda Manska

Dec. 1 19 _90_

Pay to the Order of _L & M Realty_ | $ _469.00_

and ××/100 Dollars

MADISON SAVINGS BANK

For_____ _Wanda Manska_

5.

Paula Cohen

Dec. 1 19 _90_

Pay to the Order of _Shopwell Supermarket_ | $ [ ]

Eighteen and ××/100 ___ Dollars

MADISON SAVINGS BANK

For_____ _Paula Cohen_

4 A bank teller and a customer are talking.

Listen and look at the bank slips.

Put a check (√) next to the bank slip the customer is using.

1.

DEPOSIT

Acct. # *8734569*

$150.00

2.

WITHDRAWAL

Acct. # *8734569*

$ 150.00

3.

DEPOSIT

Acct. # *8744561*

$50.00

5 Complete the sentences.

1. Your bank is closed. You need money. You go to
   a. a bank officer.
   b. an automatic teller.
   c. a bank vault.

2. You write a check. You write the amount ($25.00) on the check and
   a. in the check register.
   b. on a deposit slip.
   c. in a monthly statement.

3. You have some very important papers. You put them in a
   a. computer.
   b. cash machine.
   c. safe deposit box.

4. You are going to another country. You take
   a. your bank book.
   b. your monthly statement.
   c. traveler's checks.

5. You have to pay your rent. You don't have a checkbook. You buy a
   a. credit card.
   b. money order.
   c. withdrawal slip.

5 THE WORLD
THE UNITED STATES · CANADA

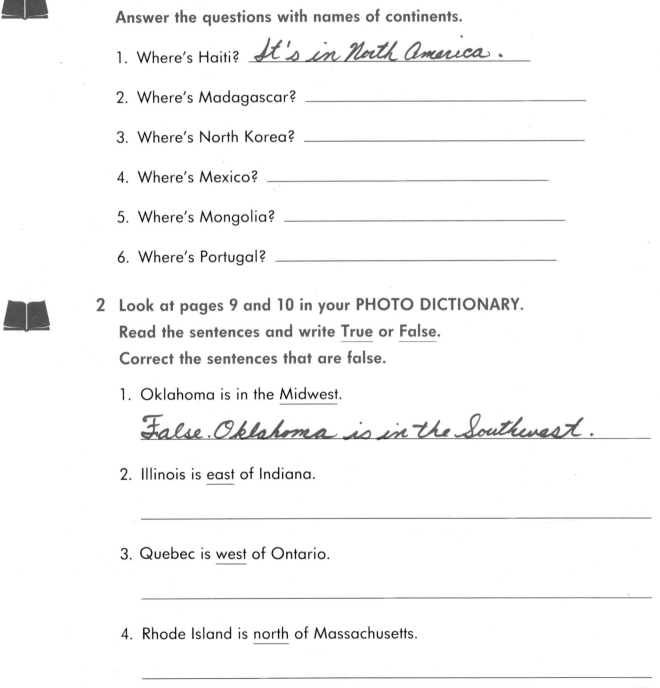

1 Look at pages 7 and 8 in your PHOTO DICTIONARY.
Answer the questions with names of continents.

1. Where's Haiti? *It's in North America.*

2. Where's Madagascar? _____

3. Where's North Korea? _____

4. Where's Mexico? _____

5. Where's Mongolia? _____

6. Where's Portugal? _____

2 Look at pages 9 and 10 in your PHOTO DICTIONARY.
Read the sentences and write True or False.
Correct the sentences that are false.

1. Oklahoma is in the Midwest.

   False. Oklahoma is in the Southwest.

2. Illinois is east of Indiana.

   _____

3. Quebec is west of Ontario.

   _____

4. Rhode Island is north of Massachusetts.

   _____

13

3 Make a list of all the countries in South America.
Put the list in alphabetical order.

List	Alphabetical Order
_____	_____
_____	_____
_____	_____
_____	_____
_____	_____
_____	_____
_____	_____
_____	_____
_____	_____
_____	_____
_____	_____
_____	_____
_____	_____
_____	_____

4 **A woman is talking to a travel agent.**
Listen and circle the word you hear.

AGENT: Where would you like to go for your vacation?

WOMAN: I'm not sure. Maybe to _____. Is a trip there very
1. Chile / (China)

expensive?

AGENT: Yes. But we have a very interesting trip to _____.
2. Austria / Australia

WOMAN: Hmmm. I don't think I want to go there. How about

_____ ?
3. Russia / Romania

AGENT: That's very expensive too. Maybe you'd enjoy a trip to

_____ .
4. Europe / Uruguay

WOMAN: I was there last year.

AGENT: Oh. How about _____ ? We have a special
5. South America / Saudi Arabia

trip to _____ . It's interesting and not very expensive.
6. Bahrain / Brazil

WOMAN: That sounds great!

6 | THE CITY

1 **Look at the pictures of 10th and 11th streets.**
   Can you find six differences?

1. There is a trash can on 10th Street.
   There isn't a trash can on 11th Street.

2. _____

_____

3. _____

_____

4. _____

_____

5. _____

_____

6. _____

_____

2 **Write five sentences about your street.**
Begin with There is(n't) or There are(n't).

1. _____

2. _____

3. _____

4. _____

5. _____

3 **Match the words in column A with the definitions in column B.**

A	B
1. _d_ skyscraper	a. a place to buy newspapers
2. ____ pedestrian	and magazines
3. ____ newsstand	b. a place to park a car
4. ____ bus stop	c. a place to put trash
5. ____ parking lot	d. a very tall building
6. ____ trash can	e. a person on the street
	f. a place to wait for a bus

17

4 **A woman is asking for directions.**

Listen and circle the word you hear.

WOMAN: Excuse me. Is there a _____ near here?
1. (newsstand) / phone booth

MAN: Yes. Walk two or three blocks. You'll see a _____ on
2. trash can / bus stop

the _____ . Turn right and walk another block. There's
3. corner / crosswalk

a _____ entrance in front of a new
4. subway / skyscraper

_____ . Go inside and you'll find it there.
5. parking lot / office building

WOMAN: Thanks a lot.

Now put a check next to the item that the woman probably wants.

☐

☐

☐

7 THE SUPERMARKET FRUIT · VEGETABLES

1 Unscramble the words.
Write them in the correct column.

1. aramgiren   *margarine*

2. cabon   _____

3. upso   _____

4. naromcai   _____

5. kilm   _____

6. zonfre nidenr   _____

7. hencick   _____

8. orytug   _____

Frozen Foods	Dairy	Canned Goods	Meats and Poultry	Packaged Goods
	margarine			

2 Juan and María are talking about dinner.

Listen and circle the word you hear.

MARÍA: Let's make _____ and cheese for dinner.
1. (macaroni) / broccoli

JUAN: Good idea! And we can have a salad too.

MARÍA: OK. What do we need?

JUAN: Well, we have _____ , but we need some _____ .
2. meat / milk   3. cheese / peaches

MARÍA: What about _____ ?
4. bread / butter

JUAN: We don't have any. We need to buy some. And we have

_____ for the salad, but we need some
5. lettuce / spinach

_____ and _____ .
6. potatoes / tomatoes   7. cucumbers / carrots

MARÍA: What do you want to drink?

JUAN: _____ juice. Do we have any?
8. Orange / Apple

MARÍA: No. We need some. What about dessert?

JUAN: Let's buy some _____ . Oh, and let's buy some
9. raspberries / strawberries

_____ too.
10. pears / bread

MARÍA: Great. Let's go to the supermarket now.

Now complete their shopping list.

To buy
macaroni

20

3 There are eight fruits and vegetables in the box.
Circle the words.
Write the words in the correct column.

L	E	M	O	N	E
O	G	V	R	O	S
N	F	P	A	C	P
I	M	A	N	O	I
O	P	L	G	R	N
N	A	H	E	N	A
I	P	U	L	T	C
R	A	D	I	S	H
B	Y	E	V	H	O
D	A	P	P	L	E

Fruits   **Vegetables**

orange   _____

_____   _____

_____   _____

_____   _____

8 THE MENU
FAST FOODS & SNACKS

Daphne's Diner

Appetizers

tomato juice	.80
fruit cup	.95
shrimp cocktail	1.25
soup (tomato, vegetable, chicken)	.75

Entrées

steak	8.45
roast beef	6.75
fish	7.50
stuffed tomatoes	4.75
pork chops	7.85
spaghetti and meatballs	5.95
roast chicken	7.85
fried chicken	7.85
hamburger	2.65
hot dog	1.25

Side Orders

tossed salad	1.25
baked potato	.95
french fries	1.05
onion rings	.95
vegetables (carrots, green beans, broccoli)	.95

Desserts

apple pie	1.50
chocolate cake	1.50
ice cream	.95
jello	.80
donut	.75

Beverages

soda	.75
milk shake	1.15
coffee	.50
tea	.50

1 Look at the menu.

Read the sentences and write <u>True</u>, <u>False</u> or <u>I don't know</u>.

Correct the statements that are false.

1. A hamburger is <u>$3.35</u>.

False. A hamburger is $2.65.

2. There are <u>two</u> kinds of potatoes.

3. Roast chicken and fried chicken are $7.85.

_____

4. There are four kinds of soup.

_____

5. The steak is very good.

_____

6. Stuffed tomatoes is an appetizer.

_____

2 You have $10.00.

Which meals can you order at Daphne's Diner?

Put a check (√) next to them.

√ 1. shrimp cocktail ____ 4. fruit cup ____ 6. vegetable soup
       fried chicken   spaghetti and   hot dog
       soda   meatballs   french fries
                                  jello   chocolate cake
____ 2. tomato juice   tea   soda
       fish
       broccoli
       ice cream   ____ 5. roast beef
       tea   baked potato
                              onion rings
____ 3. stuffed tomatoes   green beans
       french fries   apple pie
       milk shake   coffee

3 You have $13.00.

What will you order at Daphne's Diner?

_____   _____

_____   _____

_____

4 A customer is ordering a meal at Daphne's Diner.

Listen and circle the word you hear.

WAITER: Are you ready to order?

CUSTOMER: Yes. First I'd like some tomato _____ . Then I'd like the
1. juice / (soup)

_____ chicken.
2. roast / fried

WAITER: Would you like any vegetables?

CUSTOMER: _____ , please.
3. Broccoli / Carrots

WAITER: OK. Something to drink?

CUSTOMER: A cup of _____ .
4. tea / coffee

WAITER: Dessert?

CUSTOMER: Yes. I'd like some _____ .
5. apple pie / chocolate cake

WAITER: Anything else?

CUSTOMER: No, that's all, thanks.

Now complete the customer's check.

Look at the menu on page 22 and decide how much the meal is going to cost.

Check		
Tomato soup		.75
TOTAL		

9 THE POST OFFICE
THE OFFICE

1 Look at the envelope.

Read the sentences and write <u>True</u> or <u>False</u>.

Correct the sentences that are false.

Luise Mongello
20 West 68th St.
N.Y. N.Y. 10023

Miriam Shakter
9310 Euclid Street
Santa Monica, California
90403

1. The envelope has <u>one stamp</u>.

   False. The envelope has two stamps.

2. The return address is <u>9310 Euclid Street</u>.

   _____

3. Miriam's zip code is <u>9310</u>.

   _____

4. Luise's zip code is <u>10023</u>.

   _____

5. The envelope is a <u>square</u>.

   _____

2 A postal clerk and a customer are talking.

Listen and look at the pictures.

What is the man sending?

Put a check (√) next to the correct picture.

1.
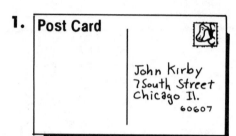

3.

2.

4.

3 Cross out the names of things you usually DON'T find on an office desk.

lamp	out box
ma̶i̶l̶box	message pad
eraser	file cabinet
secretary	stapler
paper clip holder	bulletin board
wastepaper basket	Scotch tape

4 Cross out the word that does not belong.

1. paper clip   staple   er̶a̶s̶er   rubber band

2. postal clerk   secretary   receptionist   stationery

3. envelope   pencil   typewriter   pen

4. note pad   typing paper   message pad   pencil holder

5. pencil holder   typewriter   paper clip holder   tape dispenser

10 OCCUPATIONS

1 **Match the pictures in column A with the occupations in column B.**

	A		B
1. *d*			a. dentist
2. ___			b. tailor
3. ___			c. carpenter
4. ___			d. florist
5. ___			e. nurse
6. ___			f. photographer
7. ___			g. painter

2 **Complete the sentences.**

1. A _*teller*_ works in a bank.

2. A _____ writes for a newspaper or magazine.

3. A _____ or _____ works in a restaurant.

4. A _____ works in an office.

5. A _____ works in a school.

3 Some people work inside. Some people work outside.

Put the words in the correct column.

construction worker	optometrist
ba~~k~~er	butcher
bricklayer	window washer
teller	sanitation worker

Inside

baker

_____

_____

_____

Outside

_____

_____

_____

4 Listen to the conversations.

Circle the correct answers.

1. What is the woman's occupation?
   a. Architect.
   (b.) Painter.
   c. Seamstress.

2. What is the man's occupation?
   a. Construction worker.
   b. Doctor.
   c. Teacher.

3. What is the man's occupation?
   a. Baker.
   b. Cook.
   c. Waiter.

4. What is the woman's occupation?
   a. Salesperson.
   b. Teller.
   c. Teacher.

5. What is the man's occupation?
   a. Butcher.
   b. Farmer.
   c. Florist.

6. What is the woman's occupation?
   a. Journalist.
   b. Newscaster.
   c. Teller.

7. What is the man's occupation?
   a. Dentist.
   b. Pharmacist.
   c. Veterinarian.

8. What is the woman's occupation?
   a. Police officer.
   b. Teacher.
   c. Secretary.

11 THE BODY
COSMETICS & TOILETRIES

1 Look at the picture.

   Write the correct word next to each number.

1. *nose* _____

2. _____

3. _____

4. _____

5. _____

6. _____

7. _____

8. _____

9. _____

10. _____

11. _____

12. _____

13. _____

14. _____

15. _____

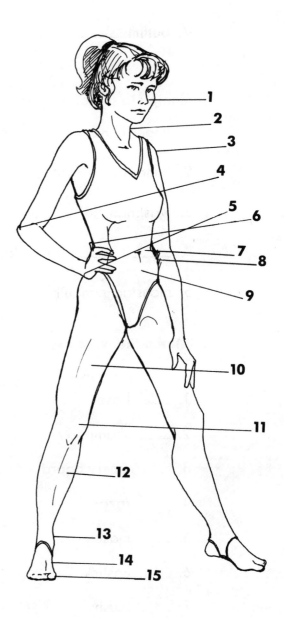

2 Unscramble the words.

Write them in the correct column.

1. yee _eye_

2. ilp _____

3. plam _____

4. hisn _____

5. eslorhud _____

6. metelp _____

7. buthm _____

Head	Arm	Hand	Leg	Foot
eye				

3 Complete the analogies.

1. finger:hand = ___toe___ :foot

2. hand:arm = foot: _____

3. wrist:hand = _____ :foot

4. _____ :arm = knee:leg

5. moustache:mouth = _____ :chin

4 Match the words in column A with the words in column B.

A	B
1. _c_ base	a. nails
2. ___ shampoo	b. eyes
3. ___ emery board	c. face
4. ___ razor	d. mouth
5. ___ mascara	e. cheeks
6. ___ lipstick	f. beard
7. ___ blush	g. hair

5 Complete the sentences.

1. Your hair is dirty. You need
   a. a brush.
   b. hair tonic.
   c. shampoo.

2. You don't want a beard or moustache. You need
   a. an emery board.
   b. an electric shaver.
   c. a nail clipper.

3. Your hair is wet. You need
   a. a hair dryer.
   b. foundation.
   c. an electric shaver.

4. You want to put color on your nails. You need
   a. a nail file.
   b. nail polish.
   c. a nail clipper.

6 A salesclerk is putting makeup on a woman.
Listen and circle the word you hear.

CLERK: OK. I finished putting the _____ on your _____ .
1. base / face   2. base / face

Now here's a little _____ for your cheeks. What would
3. brush / blush

you like on your eyes?

WOMAN: A little _____ and some _____ .
4. eyeliner / eye shadow   5. eyebrow pencil / mascara

CLERK: What about _____ ?
6. eyeliner / eye shadow

WOMAN: No thanks.

CLERK: Fine. Would you like anything else?

WOMAN: Just _____ , please.
7. lipstick / rouge

How does the woman look now? Choose the correct picture.

ACTION AT HOME
ACTION AT THE GYM
ACTION AT SCHOOL

1 **Match the pictures in column A with the words in column B.**

	A		B
1.	*f*	a.	sweep
2. ___		b.	brush your hair
3. ___		c.	take a shower
4. ___		d.	dry off
5. ___		e.	comb your hair
6. ___		f.	brush your teeth
7. ___		g.	wake up
8. ___		h.	drink
9. ___		i.	put on makeup

2 **Look at photos 1–7 on page 26 in your PHOTO DICTIONARY. Complete the paragraph about Steven Lucci.**

Every morning Steven ___*wakes up*___ at 7:00. He

_____ five minutes later. Then he
2.

_____ . After he _____ ,
3.   4.

he _____ . Then he
5.

_____ . Finally, he _____
6.   7.

and goes to work.

3 Write six sentences about what you do every day.

1. _____

2. _____

3. _____

4. _____

5. _____

6. _____

4 Read the sentences.

Look at the photos on page 26 in your **PHOTO DICTIONARY** and write True or False.

Correct the sentences that are false.

1. (photo 1) He's getting up.

   False. He's waking up. _____

2. (photo 19) She's taking a shower.

   _____

3. (photo 11) She's combing her hair.

   _____

4. (photo 10) She's putting on makeup.

   _____

5. (photo 8) She's rinsing her face.

   _____

6. (photo 17) She's watching TV.

   _____

5 Marsha Rifkin is talking about a typical morning.

Listen and match the times in column A with the actions in column B.

	A		**B**
1.	_f_ 5:30	a.	take a shower
2.	___ 6:00	b.	leave for work
3.	___ 6:30	c.	drink a cup of coffee
4.	___ 7:00	d.	eat breakfast
5.	___ 7:30	e.	bend and stretch
6.	___ 8:00	f.	get up
7.	___ 8:30	g.	watch TV

6 Match the words in column A with their opposites in column B.

	A		**B**
1.	_d_ give	a.	frown
2.	___ smile	b.	go down
3.	___ go up	c.	erase
4.	___ stand	d.	take
5.	___ write	e.	sit

13   THE DOCTOR · THE DENTIST

1   **Unscramble the words in column A.**

Match them with the words in column B.

A

1. _c_ guohc _cough_   a. aspirin

2. ___ chedeaha _____   b. braces

3. ___ boetiver _____   c. cough syrup

4. ___ trachsc _____   d. antacid

5. ___ etshcchamoa _____   e. Band-Aid

2   **Complete the sentences.**

1. You have a very bad cough. You go to see a
   a. doctor.
   b. dentist.
   c. patient.

2. The doctor listens to your heart and lungs with
   a. an x-ray.
   b. a mirror.
   c. a stethoscope.

3. The doctor wants you to take some medicine. He or she gives you
   a. an x-ray.
   b. a filling.
   c. a prescription.

4. Kleenex is the name of
   a. an adhesive tape.
   b. tissues.
   c. cough drops.

5. You have a cough. You DON'T take
   a. an antacid.
   b. cough syrup.
   c. cough drops.

6. You think you have a fever. You look for a
   a. blood pressure gauge.
   b. scale.
   c. thermometer.

3 A doctor is talking to her 10-year-old patient Jimmy.
Listen and complete the chart.

	Yes	No
1. Jimmy has a a. headache.	✓	
b. stomachache.		
c. cold.		
d. cough.		
e. fever.		
f. scratch.		
2. The doctor gives Jimmy g. some aspirin.		
h. some Kleenex.		
i. a bandage.		
j. a prescription.		

4 Cross out the names of things you usually DON'T find in a
medicine cabinet.

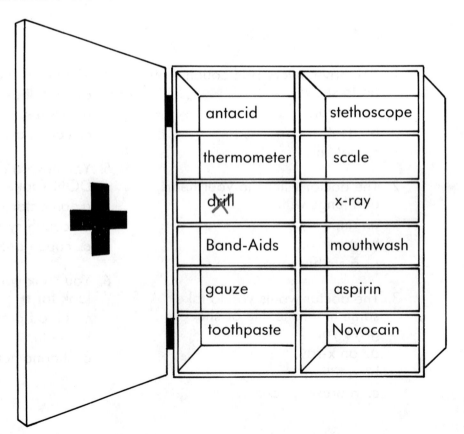

antacid   stethoscope

thermometer   scale

drill (crossed out)   x-ray

Band-Aids   mouthwash

gauze   aspirin

toothpaste   Novocain

5 Look at the form.

Read the sentences and write True, False or I don't know.

Correct the sentences that are false.

```
                Dr. Kathleen Perrone
          Eyes, Ears, Nose & Throat Specialist
                  25 East 9th Street
                 New York, N.Y. 10003
                  Tel.: (212) 555-0131

   Name  Gertrude Brooks

   Address  1087 W. 67, NY, NY
              Street        City         State
   Age    57            Date  11/11/88




   0136489              Kathleen Perrone, MD
   NYS Lic #             Prescriber's signature
```

1. This is an x-ray.

   False. It's a prescription.

2. Kathleen Perrone is a dentist.

   _____

3. Gertrude Brooks is a patient.

   _____

4. The patient has a cough.

   _____

5. Gertrude Brooks is 67 years old.

   _____

6. Dr. Perrone's office is at 25 E. 9th Street.

   _____

14 THE FAMILY

1 **Unscramble the words.**

1. fiew   *wife*

2. ons   _____

3. lenuc   _____

4. rothem   _____

5. cinee   _____

6. hafret   _____

7. wenhep   _____

8. tuna   _____

9. restis   _____

10. aurdtegh   _____

11. robhert   _____

12. dushnab   _____

2 **Look at your list in Exercise 1.**
Which are female? Which are male?
Write the words in the correct column.

Female	Male
1. *wife*	7. *son*
2. _____	8. _____
3. _____	9. _____
4. _____	10. _____
5. _____	11. _____
6. _____	12. _____

3 Look at the family tree.
Complete the sentences.

ANNA   ALFRED

JOSEPH   MARY   RICHARD   LOIS   BARRY

RACHEL   NICK   STUART

1. Alfred is Anna's ___husband___ .

2. Richard is Mary's _____ .

3. _____ is Lois's husband.

4. Joseph is Anna and Alfred's _____ .

5. Lois is Barry's _____ .

6. Nick and Stuart are _____ .

7. Richard is Rachel's _____ .

8. Rachel is Mary and Joseph's _____ .

9. Rachel, Nick and Stuart are _____ .

10. Anna and Alfred have three _____ and three

_____ .

39

4 Carol and Eric are having a dinner party.

Listen and look at the guest list.

Put a check (√) next to the people they are going to invite.

Guests

Mother √
Father
Aunt Rosa
Aunt Hilda
Uncle Herb
Uncle Sam
Cousin Ellie
Cousin Rhoda
Cousin Frank
Cousin Irene

5 Who are these people?

Complete the sentences.

1. I am the daughter of your mother's sister. I am your

   _____cousin_____ .

2. I am your father's son. I am your _____ .

3. I am the sister of your wife's brother. I am your

   _____ .

4. You have one sister. She does not have a husband. I am your sister's

   niece. I am your _____ .

15 EMOTIONS · OPPOSITES

1 Complete the sentences.

1. You don't remember a classmate's name. You feel
   a. embarrassed.
   b. pleased.
   c. bored.

2. A good friend invites you to dinner. You feel
   a. annoyed.
   b. pleased.
   c. shy.

3. You have an important test tomorrow. You feel
   a. ashamed.
   b. nervous.
   c. suspicious.

4. You are reading a book. It is not very interesting. You feel
   a. sad.
   b. bored.
   c. determined.

2 Listen to the people.

How do they feel?

Choose the correct words from the box.

scared	surprised
happy	determined
bored	furious
confused	

1. _happy_

2. _____

3. _____

4. _____

5. _____

6. _____

7. _____

3 Match the words in column A with their opposites in column B.

	A		B
1.	_g_ clean	a.	fast
2.	___ thin	b.	dry
3.	___ slow	c.	low
4.	___ high	d.	old
5.	___ young	e.	crooked
6.	___ bad	f.	thick
7.	___ wet	g.	dirty
8.	___ straight	h.	soft
9.	___ hard	i.	neat
10.	___ messy	j.	good

4 Read the sentences.

Look at the pictures and write True or False.

Correct the sentences that are false.

1. The glass is <u>full</u>.

   False. It's empty.

2. She looks <u>sad</u>.

   _____

3. The line is <u>crooked</u>.

   _____

4. It's <u>cold</u>.

   _____

5. The book is open.

_____

6. The package is light.

_____

5 **Look at the pictures.**

Complete the sentences about Joan and Anne.

Joan   **Anne**

1. _____*Joan*_____ is tall. _____*Anne*_____

_____*is*_____ short.

2. _____ is happy. _____ is

_____ .

3. Joan's hair is long and straight. Anne's hair _____

_____ and _____ .

4. Joan's dress is _____ . Anne's _____

_____ loose.

5. Joan's dress _____ dark. Anne's

dress _____ _____ .

6. Joan's belt is _____ . Anne's _____

_____ _____ .

16 MEN'S WEAR · WOMEN'S WEAR MEN'S & WOMEN'S WEAR ACCESSORIES

1 Read the list of clothes and accessories.

Put a check (√) in the correct column.

	For Men	For Women	For Men and Women
1. tie	✓		
2. boxer shorts			
3. pants			
4. blouse			
5. suit			
6. slip			
7. socks			
8. ring			
9. nightgown			
10. sneakers			
11. barrette			
12. sport shirt			

2 Complete the sentences with the names of colors.

1. The sun is *yellow* .

2. A leaf is _____ .

3. Cherries are _____ .

4. This cat  is _____ .

5. An eggplant _____ is _____ .

6. The clouds _____ are _____ .

7. This hat _____ is _____ .

3 Look at the store directory.

Read the sentences and write True or False.

Correct the sentences that are false.

<table>
<tr><td colspan="2">Store Directory</td></tr>
<tr><td>Accessories 2
   wallets, scarves,
   handbags</td><td>Men's Department 1
   suits, casual wear,
   outerwear</td></tr>
<tr><td>Jewelry Department ... 1
   rings, necklaces,
   bracelets, watches</td><td>Shoe Department 4
   shoes, boots,
   socks</td></tr>
<tr><td>Lingerie Department .. 2
   women's underwear,
   nightwear</td><td>Women's Department 3
   suits, dresses,
   casual wear, outerwear</td></tr>
</table>

1. The men's department is on the <u>second</u> floor.

False. The men's department is on the first floor.

2. The women's department is on the <u>third</u> floor.

_____

3. Wallets are on the <u>second</u> floor.

_____

4. There are nightgowns and slips in the <u>women's</u> department.

_____

5. The jewelry department is on the <u>first</u> floor.

_____

45

4 A woman wants to buy a sweater.

Listen and look at the pictures.

Put a check (✓) next to the sweater the customer wants to buy.

1.    2.    3.    4.

5 There are nine items of clothing in the box.

Circle the words.

D	E	B	B	R	A	C	L	O	N
A	N	G	L	O	V	E	S	H	E
L	I	N	O	T	S	C	A	R	F
P	S	H	U	P	N	T	O	R	G
K	I	V	S	U	I	T	M	S	G
T	P	S	E	D	S	E	M	C	H
R	M	S	H	O	L	D	E	O	P
J	D	N	P	M	I	S	E	A	D
U	N	D	E	R	P	A	N	T	S
I	K	L	D	F	S	H	O	E	S

6 Cross out the word that does not belong.

1. briefs   ~~coat~~   undershirt   socks

2. tan   purple   plaid   gray

3. tights   socks   pearls   panty hose

4. gold   diamond   topaz   ruby

5. watch   scarf   ring   necklace

6. umbrella   robe   trench coat   rain hat

17 HOUSING
THE BACKYARD AND GARDEN

1 **Look at the floor plan.**

Read the sentences and write True, False or I don't know.

Correct the sentences that are false.

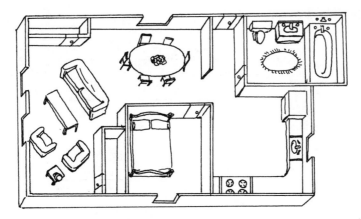

1. This is a <u>two</u>-bedroom apartment.

   False. It's a one-bedroom apartment.

2. The living room is <u>next to</u> the bedroom.

   _____

3. There are <u>five</u> windows in the apartment.

   _____

4. There <u>is</u> a small hall in the apartment.

   _____

5. This is an <u>upstairs</u> apartment.

   _____

6. There are <u>no</u> closets in the living room.

   _____

2 Cross out the word that does not belong.

1. chimney   antenna   ~~mailbox~~

2. lobby   closet   second floor

3. kitchen   bedroom   lawn

4. leaf   pansy   azalea

5. rake   barbecue   trowel

6. antenna   lounge chair   table

3 Unscramble the words.

1. osre   _____ *rose* _____

2. idasy   _____

3. lutpi   _____

4. neugrima   _____

5. alzaae   _____

6. aynsp   _____

7. gaprannsod   _____

8. fifdadlo   _____

4 Put the words in Exercise 3 in alphabetical order.

1. _____   5. _____

2. _____   6. _____

3. _____   7. _____

4. _____   8. _____

5 A woman is showing her new apartment to a friend.

Listen and look at the pictures.

Put a check (√) next to the correct floor plan.

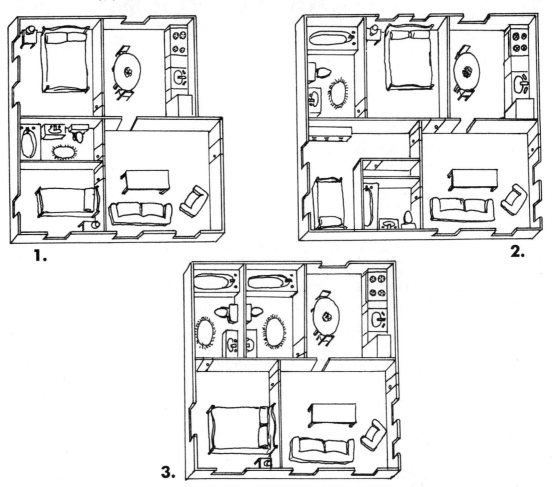

1.

2.

3.

6 Complete the sentences.

1. The car is in the
   a. chimney.
   b. closet.
   c. garage.

2. You cook in the
   a. gutter.
   b. kitchen.
   c. dining room.

3. Your apartment is on the third
   floor. You use the
   a. elevator.
   b. window.
   c. driveway.

4. You live on the second floor.
   The apartment on the first floor
   is the
   a. upstairs apartment.
   b. downstairs apartment.
   c. lobby.

5. You cook in the backyard on a
   a. hedge.
   b. wading pool.
   c. barbecue.

6. The chimney is on the
   a. roof.
   b. front walk.
   c. second floor.

18 THE LIVING ROOM THE DINING ROOM

1 Match the words in column A with the words in column B to make new words.

Write the new words in column C.

	A		B		C
1.	_C_ book	a.	piece		*bookcase*
2.	___ fire	b.	spoon		_____
3.	___ center	c.	case		_____
4.	___ arm	d.	chair		_____
5.	___ soup	e.	board		_____
6.	___ side	f.	place		_____

2 Unscramble the words.

Write them in the correct column.

		Living Room	Dining Room
1.	teapl	_____	*plate*
2.	chuoc	_____	_____
3.	totonam	_____	_____
4.	deisbrdoa	_____	_____
5.	freiclape	_____	_____
6.	kanpin	_____	_____
7.	kobosace	_____	_____

3 Look at the pictures of the two dining room tables.
Can you find eight differences?

A   **B**

1. On table A the cup is to the left of the plate.
   On table B the cup is to the right of the plate.

2. _____

   _____

3. _____

   _____

4. _____

   _____

5. _____

   _____

6. _____

   _____

7. _____

   _____

8. _____

   _____

4 A mother is telling her son how to set the table.
Listen and circle the word you hear.

MOTHER: Put the _____ on the _____ .
1. knife / (napkin)   2. plate / table

SON: Where do the _____ go?
3. forks / spoons

MOTHER: Put the _____ fork to the left of the plate. And put the
4. salad / dinner

_____ fork to the left of the dinner fork.
5. salad / dinner

SON: What about the _____ glass?
6. wine / water

MOTHER: Put it to the right of the _____ .
7. plate / cup

SON: And the _____ ?
8. knife / napkin

MOTHER: Put it to the right of the dinner plate. And put the

_____ to the right of the _____ .
9. teaspoon / soupspoon   10. teaspoon / soupspoon

And that's it!

Now complete the picture.
Draw the table items.

Legend

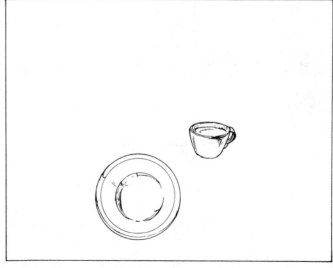

5 Complete the crossword puzzle.

Across

2 ____ the left

4 ____ are you?
Fine, thanks.

6 Daisies and tulips are ____ .

9 ____place

11 You can put your
PHOTO DICTIONARY on it.

13 What time ____ you get up?

16 The rug is on the ____ .

17 It's on a lamp.

19 A type of table.

20 It goes under a cup.

22 You can look in it.

Down

1 The opposite of yes

2 Type of pot

3 Is the living room neat
____ messy?

5 A type of glass

6 These flowers are
____ you.

7 Couches

8 You eat salad with it.

10 A color

12 ____ , fork and spoon

14 You put flowers
in them.

15 A type of seat

18 Part of the body

21 You and me

19 THE BEDROOM
THE BATHROOM

1 Match the words in column A with the words in column B.
Write the new words in column C.

A	B	C
1. _f_ pillow	a. stand	_pillowcase_
2. ___ bath	b. brush	_____
3. ___ door	c. cloth	_____
4. ___ night	d. board	_____
5. ___ wash	e. spread	_____
6. ___ tooth	f. case	_____
7. ___ head	g. tub	_____
8. ___ bed	h. knob	_____

2 Read the sentences.

Look at photos 1–8 on page 44 in your PHOTO DICTIONARY and write True or False.

Correct the sentences that are false.

1. There are <u>seven</u> towels in the bathroom.

   False. There are eight towels.

2. The <u>hand towel</u> is on the bathtub.

   _____

3. There are <u>flowers</u> on the sink.

_____

4. There is soap in the <u>soap dish</u>.

_____

Now look at photos 14–21.

5. The medicine cabinet is <u>open</u>.

_____

6. The hot water faucet <u>is</u> on.

_____

7. There are <u>three</u> toothbrushes in the toothbrush holder.

_____

3 **Complete the sentences.**

1. You need an aspirin. Look in the
   a. cup.
   b. pillowcase.
   c. medicine cabinet.

2. It's dark. Turn on the
   a. electric blanket.
   b. lamp.
   c. cold water faucet.

3. It's cold. You are in bed. You need a
   a. quilt.
   b. carpet.
   c. bath towel.

4. Wash your hands with
   a. a toothbrush.
   b. soap.
   c. a cup.

5. You are wet. You need a
   a. mirror.
   b. washcloth.
   c. bath towel.

6. Your t-shirts and sweaters are in a
   a. comforter.
   b. tub.
   c. chest.

7. A drawer has a
   a. doorknob.
   b. handle.
   c. box spring.

8. The flat sheet is
   a. on top of the fitted sheet.
   b. to the right of the fitted sheet.
   c. underneath the fitted sheet.

55

4 Look at photos 1–13 on page 43 in your PHOTO DICTIONARY.
Complete the sentences.

1. There are two white *throw pillows* on the bed.

2. The night table has three _____ .

3. There is a _____ above the dresser.

4. The _____ is blue.

5. There is a plant on the _____ .

6. There is a _____ and a

   _____ on the floor.

7. The bed has a white _____ .

5 Listen to the conversations.
Are the people in the bedroom or in the bathroom?
Put a check (√) in the correct column.

	Bedroom	Bathroom
1.	√	___
2.	___	___
3.	___	___
4.	___	___
5.	___	___
6.	___	___
7.	___	___
8.	___	___
9.	___	___
10.	___	___

20 THE KITCHEN · KITCHENWARE

1 Match the pictures in column A with the words in column B.

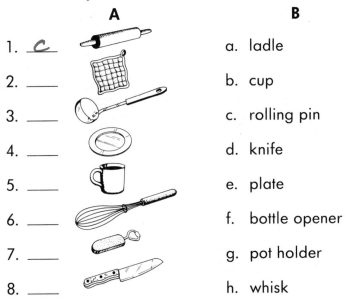

A	B
1. _c_	a. ladle
2. ___	b. cup
3. ___	c. rolling pin
4. ___	d. knife
5. ___	e. plate
6. ___	f. bottle opener
7. ___	g. pot holder
8. ___	h. whisk

2 There are seven kitchen items in the box.
Circle the words.

A	S	T	R	A	I	N	E	R
L	T	H	O	P	M	O	R	O
M	R	P	O	T	S	R	J	A
M	I	A	I	B	O	W	L	S
I	V	N	N	T	S	P	B	T
X	E	S	I	C	I	R	E	E
E	T	L	A	B	O	P	A	R
R	O	F	M	C	H	B	R	T

3 Read the recipes.

Put a check (√) next to the kitchenware you need to make pancakes and apple pie.

1. | **Pancakes**

Ingredients:

2 cups flour
3 teaspoons baking powder
1 teaspoon salt
1 tablespoon sugar
3 eggs
2 cups milk
½ cup oil

Combine flour, baking powder, salt and sugar.
Beat milk and oil into egg.
Blend with dry mix.
Cook on both sides until brown.

Kitchenware

pot	measuring cup
√ skillet	measuring spoons
roaster	can opener
bowl	egg beater
rolling pin	knife
spatula	grater

2. | **Apple Pie**

Ingredients:

6-8 apples
½ cup sugar
¼ teaspoon cinnamon
½ teaspoon butter
2 teaspoons lemon juice

Peel and cut apples into thin slices.
Fill 8" pie crust with apples and rest of ingredients. Bake at 350°F.

Kitchenware

measuring cup	can opener
cookie sheet	knife
rolling pin	strainer
measuring spoons	peeler
blender	spatula

4 Cross out the word that does not belong.

1. sink   dishwasher   ~~drawer~~

2. plastic wrap   dish towel   aluminum foil

3. stove   microwave oven   roaster

4. blender   grater   mixer

5. cake pan   cookie sheet   spatula

6. dishwasher   refrigerator   ladle

5 Lisa and Irving are making breakfast.
Listen and circle the word you hear.

LISA: Where's the coffee _____ ?
                    1. cup / (pot)

IRVING: I don't have one. I have a coffee _____ . It's on the
                                                         2. maker / pot

           _____ next to the _____ .
           3. counter / canister   4. sink / whisk

LISA: OK. And where's the _____ ?
                                    5. roaster / toaster

IRVING: To the right of the _____ . Anything else?
                                6. bowl / stove

LISA: Bread.

IRVING: Oh, it's in the _____ . And I'll get the
                          7. refrigerator / canister

           _____ .
           8. cups / pots

LISA: Good. And don't forget the _____ .
                                        9. plates / grater

59

21 THE NURSERY THE PLAYGROUND

1 Which things can you usually find in the nursery? At the playground? Put a check (√) in the correct column.

	Nursery	Playground
1. swing	____	✓
2. playpen	____	____
3. bench	____	____
4. water fountain	____	____
5. highchair	____	____
6. crib	____	____
7. jungle gym	____	____
8. see-saw	____	____
9. slide	____	____
10. rug	____	____

2 Write the names of five nursery or playground things that have wheels.

1. _stroller_

2. _____

3. _____

4. _____

5. _____

3 Where are the children?

Fill in the blanks with <u>in</u> or <u>on</u>.

1. _on_ the changing pad

2. _____ the crib

3. _____ the bench

4. _____ the sandbox

5. _____ the skateboard

6. _____ the highchair

7. _____ the rug

8. _____ the see-saw

4 Listen to the conversations.

Are the people in the nursery or at the playground?

Put a check (√) in the correct column.

	Nursery	Playground
1.	___	√
2.	___	___
3.	___	___
4.	___	___
5.	___	___
6.	___	___
7.	___	___
8.	___	___
9.	___	___
10.	___	___

22 THE LAUNDRY ROOM
TOOLS · CONSTRUCTION

1 Match the pictures in column A with the words in column B.

A **B**

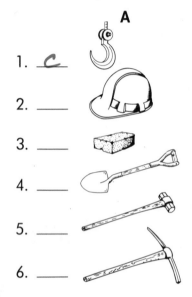

1. _c_   a. hard hat

2. ___   b. shovel

3. ___   c. hook

4. ___   d. sledge hammer

5. ___   e. pick ax

6. ___   f. brick

2 Match the words in column A and the words in column B to make new words.

Write the new words in column C.

A	B	C
1. _e_ tool	a. driver	_toolbox_
2. ___ clothes	b. paper	_____
3. ___ paint	c. hoe	_____
4. ___ screw	d. bench	_____
5. ___ sand	e. box	_____
6. ___ work	f. line	_____
7. ___ back	g. brush	_____

3 What do you need for the job?

Put a check (√) next to the items.

1. Wash your clothes.
   - _____ a. sponge
   - __√__ b. detergent
   - _____ c. bulb
   - _____ d. bucket
   - __√__ e. washer

2. Dry your clothes.
   - _____ a. hamper
   - _____ b. ironing board
   - _____ c. clothesline
   - _____ d. hanger
   - _____ e. crane

3. Wash the bathroom floor.
   - _____ a. dustpan
   - _____ b. mop
   - _____ c. vacuum cleaner
   - _____ d. bucket
   - _____ e. trowel

4. Paint your living room ceiling.
   - _____ a. paint
   - _____ b. sandpaper
   - _____ c. roller
   - _____ d. ladder
   - _____ e. mop

5. Hang a picture.
   - _____ a. screw
   - _____ b. square
   - _____ c. nail
   - _____ d. scaffold
   - _____ e. hammer

4 Read the sentences.

Look at photos 15–22 on page 49 in your PHOTO DICTIONARY and circle the correct answer.

1. The hamper is (full) / empty.

2. The dryer is open / closed.

3. The detergent is on the washer / dryer.

4. The laundry basket / laundry bag is in front of the dryer.

5. The hamper is white / red.

6. The measuring cup is in front of / behind the detergent.

7. The dryer is to the left of / to the right of the washing machine.

5 A salesperson and a customer are talking.
Listen and circle the word you hear.

SALESPERSON: Can I help you?

CUSTOMER: Yes. I need a _____ and _____ drill,
1. (saw) / cord   2. an electric / a hand

please.

SALESPERSON: OK. Anything else?

CUSTOMER: Yes. Some _____ and a _____ .
3. hooks / screws   4. paint roller / paintbrush

SALESPERSON: Do you need paint too?

CUSTOMER: No. I have a _____ .
5. can / pan

SALESPERSON: Anything else?

CUSTOMER: No, that's all, thanks.

Now circle the correct answer to this question.

What is the woman going to do?
a. Wash clothes.
b. Mop the bathroom floor.
c. Build and paint a desk.
d. Paint a picture.

23 ELECTRONICS

1 Which machines use cassettes?
Put a check (✓) next to them.

_____ 1. TV

✓ 2. VCR

_____ 3. amplifier

_____ 4. tape deck

_____ 5. CD

_____ 6. tape recorder

_____ 7. Walkman

_____ 8. computer

_____ 9. answering machine

_____ 10. pocket calculator

2 There are eight pieces of electronic equipment in the box. Circle the words.

A	C	A	L	C	U	L	A	T	O	R
P	O	R	X	A	V	O	N	F	G	L
M	M	T	V	A	V	J	E	L	O	P
E	P	U	C	A	M	E	R	A	Y	S
A	U	N	R	E	M	I	A	S	O	U
A	T	E	B	J	X	R	D	H	O	M
L	E	R	S	M	A	T	I	S	P	B
O	R	K	D	E	L	G	O	V	I	P

3 There are eight mistakes in the computer printout.

Circle the incorrect words.

Write the correct words below.

```
○
○   (casette)        computer         batery
○   television       key board        tap recorder
○   flash            calculator       record
○   skreen           kamera           lens
○   headfone         film             slide progector
○
○
```

1. _cassette_   5. _____

2. _____   6. _____

3. _____   7. _____

4. _____   8. _____

4 Listen to the sounds.

Which machines make them?

Choose a machine from the words in the box.

```
radio          answering machine
TV             typewriter
telephone✗     record player
camera
```

1. _telephone_   5. _____

2. _____   6. _____

3. _____   7. _____

4. _____

24 LAND & WATER

1 Unscramble the words.

Put a check (√) in the correct column.

		Land	Water
1. lilh	*hill*	√	___
2. reet	_____	___	___
3. donp	_____	___	___
4. uned	_____	___	___
5. kale	_____	___	___
6. vierr	_____	___	___

2 Where are the people?

Circle the correct answers.

1. (lake)   waterfall   (pond)   brook

2. mountain   hill   desert   dunes

3. meadow   lake   river   field

4. field   cliff   forest   desert

5. pond   lake   waterfall   cliff

3 Circle the correct answer.

1. Grass is (green) / red.

2. The desert is <u>dry</u> / wet.

3. There are dunes in a <u>valley</u> / desert.

4. A rock is <u>hard</u> / soft.

5. A stream is a <u>waterfall</u> / brook.

6. A forest is <u>light</u> / dark.

7. A mountain is <u>high</u> / low.

8. A valley is <u>high</u> / low.

4 Look at the picture.

Read the sentences and write <u>True</u> or <u>False</u>.

Correct the sentences that are false.

1. There are <u>three</u> trees in the picture.

False. There are two trees in the picture.

2. There are <u>rocks</u> to the right of the trees.

_____

3. There is a <u>mountain</u> behind the meadow.

_____

4. There is a <u>stream</u> to the left of the trees.

_____

5 Listen to the radio commercial.

Put a check (√) next to the correct travel poster.

1.

2.

3.

25 THE CAR

1 Look at the picture.

Write the correct word or words next to each number.

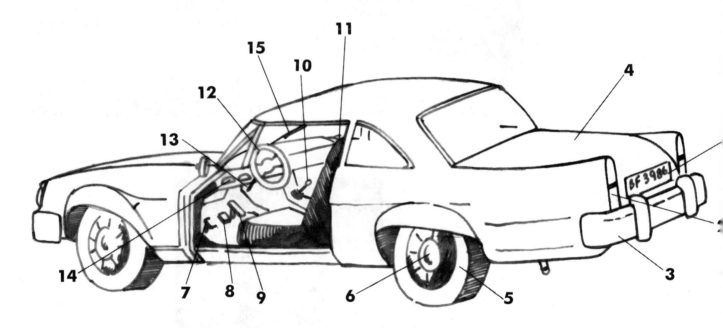

1. *license plate*

2. _____

3. _____

4. _____

5. _____

6. _____

7. _____

8. _____

9. _____

10. _____

11. _____

12. _____

13. _____

14. _____

15. _____

2 Read the sentences.

Look at the car in Exercise 1 and write True or False.

Correct the sentences that are false.

1. The license plate number is BF 2986.

False. The license plate number is BF 3986.

2. The clutch is to the left of the brake.

_____

3. The car is new.

_____

4. It's a convertible.

_____

5. The turn signal is to the left of the steering wheel.

_____

3 You are in a car.

Complete the sentences.

1. Stop the car! Use the
   a. gas pedal.
   b. ignition.
   c. brake. *(circled)*

2. Start the car. Turn on the
   a. speedometer.
   b. windshield wipers.
   c. ignition.

3. It's raining. Use the
   a. heater hose.
   b. radiator.
   c. windshield wipers.

4. You are cold. Turn on the
   a. heater.
   b. temperature gauge.
   c. radiator.

5. Is there gas in the car? Look at the
   a. temperature gauge.
   b. fuel gauge.
   c. gas pedal.

6. The gas pedal is the
   a. gas pump.
   b. clutch.
   c. accelerator.

4 A woman is talking to a police officer.

Which car did the woman see?

Listen and put a check (√) next to the correct car.

1.

2.

3.

4.

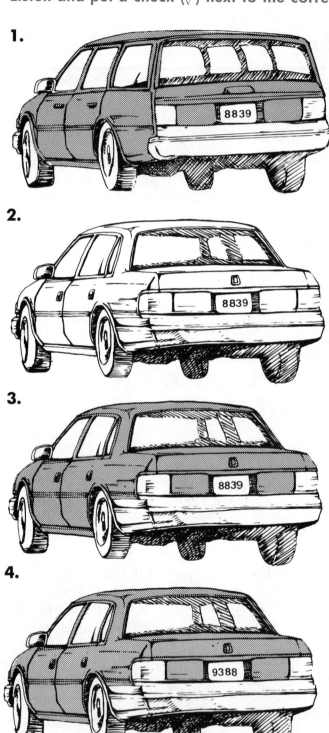

26 THE TRAIN, BUS & TAXI

1 **Look at the train schedule.**
Answer the questions.

WHITE PLAINS TO NEW YORK					
MONDAY TO FRIDAY, EXCEPT HOLIDAYS					
Leave	Arrive	Leave	Arrive	Leave	Arrive
White Plains	New York	White Plains	New York	White Plains	New York
AM	AM	AM	AM	PM	PM
12:07	12:52	9:26E	10:01	4:02E	4:37
5:03	5:45	9:37	10:22	4:07L	4:56
5:23L	6:10	10:02E	10:37	4:37	5:22
5:53L	6:40	10:07L	10:56	5:02E	5:37
6:24	7:09	10:37	11:22	5:07L	5:55
6:34E	7:11	11:02E	11:37	5:37L	6:25
6:46	7:30	11:07L	11:55	6:02E	6:37
6:55E	7:33	11:37	12:22	6:07L	6:57
7:12E	7:51	12:02E	12:37	6:37	7:22
7:21E	7:56	12:07L	12:55	7:02E	7:37
7:25E	8:00	12:37	1:22	7:07L	7:55
7:43E	8:18	1:02E	1:37	8:02E	8:37
7:46E	8:21	1:07L	1:55	8:07L	8:55
8:03E	8:37	1:37	2:22	9:02E	9:37
8:23E	8:58	2:02E	2:37	9:07L	9:55
8:26E	9:01	2:07L	2:55	10:02E	10:37
8:30E	9:10	2:37	3:22	10:07L	10:55
8:44E	9:24	3:02E	3:37	11:07	11:52
8:53E	9:27	3:07L	3:55	12:07	12:52
9:00E	9:38	3:37	4:22	....	....
AM	AM	PM	PM	AM	AM
SATURDAY, SUNDAY & HOLIDAYS					
AM	AM	AM	AM	PM	PM
12:07	12:52	11:02E	11:37	6:02E	6:37
5:37	6:22	11:07	11:52	6:07L	6:55
6:37L	7:25	12:02E	12:37	7:02E	7:37
7:07L	7:55	12:07L	12:55	7:07	7:52
7:37	8:22	1:07	1:53	8:02E	8:37
8:02E	8:37	2:02E	2:37	8:07L	8:55
8:07L	8:55	2:07L	2:55	9:07	9:52
8:37	9:22	3:07	3:53	10:02E	10:37
9:02E	9:37	4:02E	4:37	10:07L	10:55
9:07L	9:55	4:07L	4:55	11:07	11:52
10:02E	10:37	5:02E	5:37	12:07	12:52
10:07L	10:55	5:07	5:53	....	....
AM	AM	PM	PM	AM	AM

1. It is Monday. The 9:26 A.M. train arrives in New York at ___10:01___ .

2. It is Tuesday. The 4:02 P.M. train arrives in New York at _____ .

3. It is Wednesday. The first train to New York leaves White Plains at

_____ .

4. It is Saturday. The 10:02 A.M. train arrives in New York at _____ .

5. It is Sunday. The second train to New York leaves at _____ .

6. It is Christmas. The 6:02 P.M. train arrives in New York at _____ .

2 You are at the train station.

Complete the sentences.

1. You want a train ticket. Go to the
   a. information booth.
   b. red cap.
   ⓒ ticket counter.

2. What time is it? Look at the
   a. arrival and departure board.
   b. platform.
   c. clock.

3. Your suitcase is heavy. Look for a
   a. porter.
   b. passenger.
   c. ticket counter.

4. Your train leaves from track 9 at 5:00. It is 4:55. Go to the
   a. clock.
   b. platform.
   c. information booth.

5. You are on a bus. Your suitcase is
   a. in the passenger car.
   b. in the luggage compartment.
   c. on the track.

6. A _____ has four doors.
   a. train
   b. bus
   c. taxi

7. A redcap is a
   a. porter.
   b. driver.
   c. passenger.

8. You want a taxi. Go to the
   a. ticket counter.
   b. bus station.
   c. taxi stand.

3 Look at photo C on page 56 in your PHOTO DICTIONARY. Read the sentences and write True or False.

Correct the sentences that are false.

1. The taxi is red.

   False. The taxi is yellow.

2. The trunk is open.

   _____

3. The door is open.

   _____

4. The off-duty sign is on.

   _____

5. The taxi is <u>old</u> and <u>dirty</u>.

_____

6. The license plate number is <u>9003 TD</u>.

_____

4 **A man is talking to an agent at an information booth.**
Listen and circle the word you hear.

MAN: Is that _____ correct?
                   1. (clock) / schedule

AGENT: Yes. It's 4:30.

MAN: What time does the _____ to Philadelphia leave?
                                   2. train / bus

AGENT: At 5:00.

MAN: And where can I get a _____ ?
                            3. ticket / porter

AGENT: At the _____ over there.
                 4. track / counter

MAN: I see. And what is the _____ number?
                         5. taxi / track

AGENT: Look at the _____ for that information, please.
               6. schedule / departure board

MAN: OK. And can I have a _____ ?
                     7. schedule / suitcase

AGENT: Here you are.

MAN: Thank you very much.

Now complete the sentence.

The man is going to Philadelphia
by _____ .
a. bus.
b. train.
c. airplane.

27 ROUTES & ROAD SIGNS

1 Match the signs in column A with the words in column B.

	A		B

A **B**

1. *f*   a. no right turn

2. ___   b. hill

3. ___    c. no U-turn

4. ___   d. curve

5. ___    e. school crossing

6. ___   f. telephone

7. ___   g. route sign

8. ___   h. slippery when wet

9. ___   i. no left turn

10. ___   j. no trucks

2 Look at photos 1–4 on page 57 in your PHOTO DICTIONARY.
Read the sentences and write True or False.
Correct the sentences that are false.

1. There are <u>four</u> cars in the photo.

   False. There are six cars in the photo.

2. There <u>is</u> a bus in the photo.

   _____

3. There is a <u>route sign</u> in the photo.

   _____

4. The red car is driving on the <u>underpass</u>.

   _____

5. The speed limit is <u>55</u>.

   _____

Now look at photos 5–13.

6. Car number 11 is in the <u>left</u> lane.

   _____

7. There are <u>no</u> cars on the shoulder.

   _____

8. There <u>is</u> a traffic light on the highway.

   _____

9. There <u>is</u> grass on the divider.

   _____

10. There is a <u>double yellow line</u> on the highway.

   _____

3 A woman is talking to a police officer.

Listen and look at the map.

Where is the post office?

Put a check (√) next to the correct number.

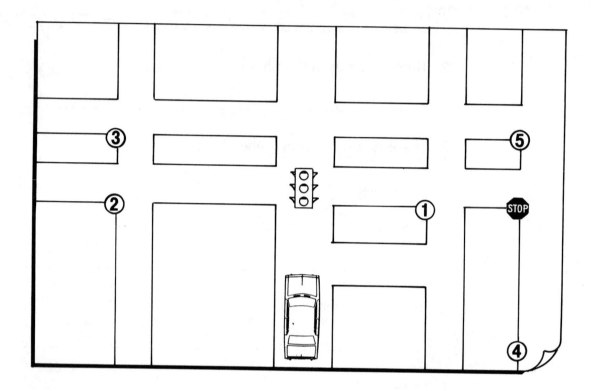

28 THE AIRPORT

1 **Which can you usually find in the terminal? On the runway? On board? Put a check (√) in the correct column.**

	Terminal	Runway	On Board
1. security check	√	—	—
2. cockpit	—	—	—
3. helicopter	—	—	—
4. baggage claim area	—	—	—
5. gate	—	—	—
6. co-pilot	—	—	—
7. jet	—	—	—
8. flight attendant	—	—	—

2 **Cross out the word that does not belong.**

1. ticket agent   passenger   customs officer   ticket ~~counter~~
2. wing   jet engine   luggage carrier   tail
3. window seat   middle seat   aisle seat   cockpit
4. boarding pass   passport   tray   ticket
5. waiting room   gate   cabin   cockpit

3 You are at the airport.
Put the steps in the correct order.

_____ gate

_____ customs

_____ jet

_____ baggage claim area

_____ security check

___/___ check-in counter

_____ waiting room

4 Look at pages 59–60 in your PHOTO DICTIONARY.
There are seven names of occupations.
Write the words here.

1. _ticket agent_

2. _____

3. _____

4. _____

5. _____

6. _____

7. _____

5 A passenger is talking to a ticket agent at the airport.

Listen and look at the seating plan.

Put a check (√) next to the passenger's boarding pass.

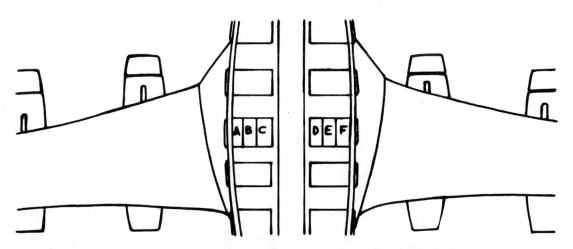

1.

ISSUED BY

NORTHEASTERN
BOARDING PASS

| NAME OF PASSENGER |
| ORTIZ / V. |

| FROM |
| PITTSBURGH PA. |
| TO |
| MIAMI FL. |

CARRIER
NORTHEASTERN

| FLIGHT | CLASS | DATE | TIME |
| NE 345Y | 49 | APR | 10:00 |

| SEAT |
| 13F |

3.

ISSUED BY

NORTHEASTERN
BOARDING PASS

| NAME OF PASSENGER |
| ORTIZ / V. |

| FROM |
| PITTSBURGH PA. |
| TO |
| MIAMI FL. |

CARRIER
NORTHEASTERN

| FLIGHT | CLASS | DATE | TIME |
| NE 345Y | 49 | APR | 10:00 |

| SEAT |
| 13E |

2.

ISSUED BY

NORTHEASTERN
BOARDING PASS

| NAME OF PASSENGER |
| ORTIZ / V. |

| FROM |
| PITTSBURGH PA. |
| TO |
| MIAMI FL. |

CARRIER
NORTHEASTERN

| FLIGHT | CLASS | DATE | TIME |
| NE 345Y | 49 | APR | 10:00 |

| SEAT |
| 13D |

4.

ISSUED BY

NORTHEASTERN
BOARDING PASS

| NAME OF PASSENGER |
| ORTIZ / V. |

| FROM |
| PITTSBURGH PA. |
| TO |
| MIAMI FL. |

CARRIER
NORTHEASTERN

| FLIGHT | CLASS | DATE | TIME |
| NE 345Y | 49 | APR | 9:00 |

| SEAT |
| 13C |

29 THE WATERFRONT · THE BEACH

1 Unscramble the words.

Put a check (√) in the correct column.

		Waterfront	Beach
1. brorah	*harbor*	√	___
2. nasd	_____	___	___
3. dobarlawk	_____	___	___
4. okdc	_____	___	___
5. brelalum	_____	___	___
6. filedrgua	_____	___	___
7. glonroeshnam	_____	___	___
8. nearc	_____	___	___
9. shealesl	_____	___	___
10. ancoe	_____	___	___

2 Cross out the word that does not belong.

1. pail   ball   ~~umbrella~~   5. blanket   sand   towel

2. lifeguard   longshoreman   hotel   6. trashcan   bucket   rock

3. sand castle   rock   seashell   7. umbrella   bathing suit   hat

4. ferry   tugboat   wave   8. harbor   ocean   tanker

3 Where are the lifeguards?

Fill in the blanks with <u>in</u>, <u>on</u> or <u>under</u>.

1. _____on_____ a barge

2. _____ the beach

3. _____ the ocean

4. _____ a beach umbrella

5. _____ a beach blanket

6. _____ the boardwalk

7. _____ a hotel

8. _____ the pier

4 Are the people at the waterfront or at the beach?

Listen and put a check (√) in the correct column.

	Waterfront	Beach
1.	√	___
2.	___	___
3.	___	___
4.	___	___
5.	___	___
6.	___	___
7.	___	___
8.	___	___

30 WATER SPORTS WINTER SPORTS

1 **Read the sentences.**

Look at the pictures and write True or False.

Correct the sentences that are false.

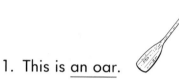

1. This is <u>an oar</u>.

False. It's a paddle.

2. This is an <u>air tank</u>.

_____

3. This is <u>a ski boot</u>.

_____

4. This is a <u>ski cap</u>.

_____

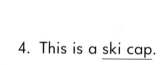

5. A <u>skier</u> uses this.

_____

6. A <u>kayaker</u> uses this.

_____

7. This is a <u>sled</u>.

_____

8. This is a <u>wet suit</u>.

_____

2 Which is a water sport? A winter sport?
   Put a check (√) in the correct column.

	Water Sports	Winter Sports
1. sledding	____	√
2. surfing	____	____
3. rowing	____	____
4. figure skating	____	____
5. snorkeling	____	____
6. downhill skiing	____	____
7. snowmobiling	____	____
8. diving	____	____

3 Match the words in column A with the words in column B.

A	B
1. _e_ swimmer	a. ice
2. ____ downhill skier	b. line
3. ____ skater	c. paddle
4. ____ fisherman	d. towrope
5. ____ windsurfer	e. pool
6. ____ water-skier	f. sail
7. ____ rower	g. wet suit
8. ____ cross country skier	h. chair lift
9. ____ scuba diver	i. trail
10. ____ canoeist	j. oar

4 **Look at pages 63–64 in your PHOTO DICTIONARY.**
Answer the questions.

1. Which sports use a boat?

   a. _sailing_

   b. _____

   c. _____

   d. _____

   e. _____

   f. _____

2. Which sports use a mask?

   a. _____

   b. _____

   c. _____

3. Which sports use a helmet?

   a. _____

   b. _____

   c. _____

4. Which sports use poles?

   a. _____

   b. _____

5. Which sports use skis?

   a. _____

   b. _____

   c. _____

5 **Listen and circle the correct sport.**

1. (a.) surfing
   b. windsurfing
   c. kayaking

2. a. white water rafting
   b. scuba diving
   c. skiing

3. a. fishing
   b. kayaking
   c. white water rafting

4. a. canoeing
   b. kayaking
   c. rowing

5. a. waterskiing
   b. downhill skiing
   c. cross country skiing

6. a. waterskiing
   b. sailing
   c. sledding

31 SPECTATOR SPORTS OTHER SPORTS

1 Match the pictures in column A with the words in column B.

	A		B
_c_ 1.			a. tennis ball
_____ 2.			b. golf ball
_____ 3.			c. baseball
_____ 4.			d. football
_____ 5.			e. volleyball
_____ 6.			f. basketball
_____ 7.			g. bowling ball
_____ 8.			h. ping pong ball

2 Which words are for people?
Put a check (√) next to them.

✓ 1. coach   _____ 6. cyclist

_____ 2. goalie   _____ 7. roller skate

_____ 3. stirrup   _____ 8. umpire

_____ 4. gutter   _____ 9. spectator

_____ 5. backpack   _____ 10. halfback

87

3   Complete the sentences.

1. An archer uses a bow and
   a. ball.
   b. net.
   (c.) arrow.

2. A roller skater skates
   a. on ice.
   b. on a field.
   c. in a rink.

3. A _____ player does NOT use a racket.
   a. tennis
   b. handball
   c. squash

4. _____ does NOT use a ball.
   a. Karate
   b. Squash
   c. Bowling

5. There are only two people in
   a. ice hockey.
   b. wrestling.
   c. volleyball.

6. You play _____ on a field.
   a. hockey
   b. tennis
   c. soccer

7. Ping pong is
   a. table tennis.
   b. volleyball.
   c. tennis.

8. A quarterback plays
   a. basketball.
   b. football.
   c. baseball.

9. _____ is heavy.
   a. A ping pong ball
   b. An arrow
   c. A bowling ball

10. A _____ has two wheels.
    a. backpack
    b. bike
    c. horse

11. _____ does NOT use a net.
    a. Ping pong
    b. Tennis
    c. Squash

12. _____ DON'T need a uniform.
    a. Hockey players
    b. Football players
    c. Joggers

4 There are six sports words in the baseball diamond.
Circle the words.

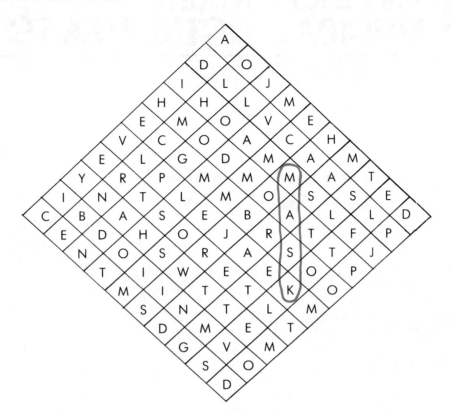

5 Listen and circle the correct sport.

1. a. basketball
   b. football
   c. baseball

2. a. ping pong
   b. tennis
   c. handball

3. a. basketball
   b. football
   c. baseball

4. a. ping pong
   b. tennis
   c. handball

5. a. karate
   b. cycling
   c. camping

6. a. ping pong
   b. bowling
   c. archery

7. a. jogging
   b. rollerskating
   c. golf

8. a. golf
   b. archery
   c. hiking

9. a. camping
   b. handball
   c. horseback riding

10. a. wrestling
    b. boxing
    c. karate

32 ENTERTAINMENT MUSICAL INSTRUMENTS

1 Unscramble the musical instruments.
Put a check (√) in the correct column.

		Brass	Percussion	Strings	Woodwinds
1. buta	*tuba*	√	___	___	___
2. tulfe	_____	___	___	___	___
3. rumd	_____	___	___	___	___
4. tugair	_____	___	___	___	___
5. booe	_____	___	___	___	___
6. lovini	_____	___	___	___	___
7. lolec	_____	___	___	___	___
8. bymlac	_____	___	___	___	___
9. larcine	_____	___	___	___	___
10. ososnab	_____	___	___	___	___

2 Cross out the names of things you usually DON'T find on a stage.

chorus	singer
billboard	aisle
audience	ballerina
actress	footlights
marquee	orchestra pit

**3 Read the sentences and write True or False.
Correct the sentences that are false.**

1. A ballerina stands on a podium.

    False. A ballerina stands on a stage.

2. A vocalist wears toe shoes.

    _____

3. An actor works in the theater.

    _____

4. A xylophone is a percussion instrument.

    _____

5. The saxophone is a brass instrument.

    _____

6. An audience sits in a theater.

    _____

7. A conductor works with a symphony orchestra.

    _____

8. A violin is brown.

    _____

9. There are singers in a chorus.

    _____

10. There are footlights on the music stand.

    _____

4 What do you hear?

Listen and circle the correct answer.

1. (a.) orchestra
   b. drum
   c. chorus

2. a. opera singer
   b. rock singer
   c. chorus

3. a. opera singer
   b. rock singer
   c. chorus

4. a. chorus
   b. rock singer
   c. opera singer

5. a. vocalist
   b. opera singer
   c. rock singer

6. a. conductor
   b. audience
   c. actor

7. a. singer
   b. actress
   c. actor

8. a. piano
   b. xylophone
   c. orchestra

9. a. cymbal
   b. trumpet
   c. drum

10. a. violin
    b. trumpet
    c. flute

5 Complete the crossword puzzle.

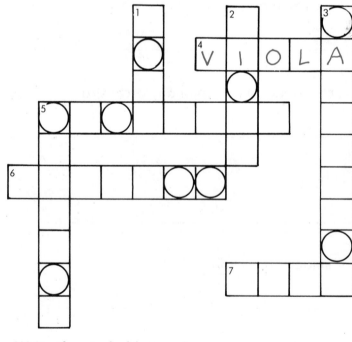

Write the circled letters here.

_____ _____ _____ _____ _____ _____ _____ _____

Across

4.

5.

6.

7.

Down

1.

2.

3.

5.

33 THE ZOO & PETS

1 Look at the picture.
   Write the correct word next to each number.

1. _mane_

2. _____

3. _____

4. _____

What animal is this? _____

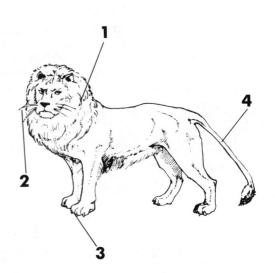

2 Match the words in column A with the words in column B.

	A		B
1. _f_	elephant	a.	spots
2. ___	leopard	b.	whiskers
3. ___	lion	c.	pouch
4. ___	cat	d.	horns
5. ___	camel	e.	stripes
6. ___	kangaroo	f.	trunk
7. ___	rhinoceros	g.	hump
8. ___	tiger	h.	mane

3 Unscramble the animals.

Put a check (√) in the correct column.

		Zoo	Home
1. ogd	*dog*	___	√
2. cleam	_____	___	___
3. xof	_____	___	___
4. kraepeat	_____	___	___
5. tramesh	_____	___	___
6. lilarog	_____	___	___
7. sholdifg	_____	___	___
8. malla	_____	___	___
9. popsumipthoa	_____	___	___

4 Name the animals.

1. A _*tiger*_ and a _*zebra*_ have stripes.

2. A _____ has a very long neck.

3. An _____ has very big ears.

4. A _____ has horns.

5. A _____ and a _____ can jump.

6. A _____ has black and white stripes.

7. A _____ is very slow.

8. A _____ is a baby dog.

9. A _____ is a baby cat.

10. A _____ lives in a bowl.

5 Complete the analogies.

1. puppy:dog = ____*kitten*____ :cat

2. stripes:tiger = spots: _____

3. tusks:elephant = _____ :rhinoceros

4. horn:buffalo = antler: _____

5. _____ :slow = tiger:fast

6. camel:hump = _____ :pouch

7. polar bear: _____ = gorilla:black

8. lion:zoo = _____ :home

6 Listen to the sounds.

What animals make them?

Circle the correct answer.

1. a. dog
   b. elephant
   c. lion

2. a. parakeet
   b. cat
   c. snake

3. a. dog
   b. lion
   c. bear

4. a. parakeet
   b. parrot
   c. rabbit

5. a. bear
   b. dog
   c. fox

6. a. tiger
   b. dog
   c. cat

7. a. parakeet
   b. kitten
   c. parrot

34 THE FARM
FISH & SEA ANIMALS

1 Look at the picture.

Read the sentences and write <u>True</u> or <u>False</u>.

Correct the sentences that are false.

1. This is a <u>zoo</u>.

   False. It's a farm.

2. There is a <u>lake</u> to the right of the farmhouse.

   _____

3. There are <u>chickens</u> in front of the farmhouse.

   _____

4. There <u>is</u> a tractor on the farm.

   _____

5. The tractor is next to the <u>silo</u>.

   _____

6. There are three <u>bulls</u> on the farm.

   _____

7. The <u>silo</u> is to the right of the barn.

_____

8. The farmer is on the <u>tractor</u>.

_____

2 Match the words in column A with the words in column B.

	A		**B**
_d_	1. chicken	a.	calf
____	2. cow	b.	kid
____	3. pig	c.	lamb
____	4. goat	d.	chick
____	5. sheep	e.	piglet

3 Complete the sentences.

1. A shark has
   a. tentacles.
   b. claws.
   (c.) fins.

2. An angelfish has
   a. spots.
   b. stripes.
   c. flippers.

3. _____ does NOT have a
   shell.
   a. A clam
   b. A mussel
   c. An octopus

4. A _____ is very big.
   a. trout
   b. whale
   c. starfish

5. A _____ does NOT
   have gills.
   a. lobster
   b. bass
   c. trout

6. A _____ does NOT
   have claws.
   a. crab
   b. clam
   c. lobster

7. _____ has tentacles.
   a. A crab
   b. An octopus
   c. A starfish

4 Which animal names are male? Which are female? Which can be male or female?

Put a check (√) in the correct column.

	Male	Female	Male or Female
1. rooster	√	___	___
2. sheep	___	___	___
3. hen	___	___	___
4. horse	___	___	___
5. goat	___	___	___
6. bull	___	___	___
7. kid	___	___	___
8. pig	___	___	___
9. cow	___	___	___
10. lamb	___	___	___

5 Listen to the sounds.

Which animals make them?

Circle the correct answer.

1. a. pig
   b. bull
   c. calf

2. a. kid
   b. chicken
   c. horse

3. a. goat
   b. cow
   c. horse

4. a. piglet
   b. cow
   c. horse

5. a. lamb
   b. pig
   c. goat

6. a. hen
   b. rooster
   c. horse

35 BIRDS · INSECTS & RODENTS

1 Name the birds.

Use the words in the box.

cockatoo	owl
crane	pelican
duck	pigeon
~~eagle~~	swan

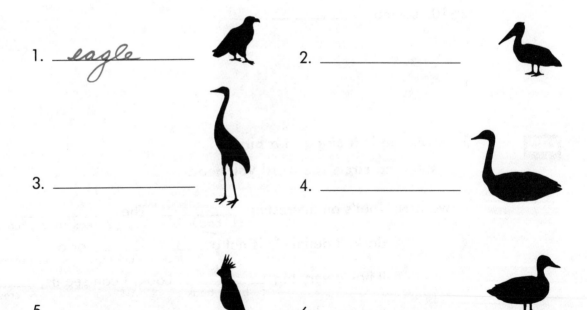

1. *eagle* _____

2. _____

3. _____

4. _____

5. _____

6. _____

7. _____

8. _____

99

2 Unscramble the words.

Put a check (√) in the correct column.

		Birds	Insects	Rodents
1. wol	_owl_	√	___	___
2. ebe	_____	___	___	___
3. boirn	_____	___	___	___
4. risquler	_____	___	___	___
5. qusomtoi	_____	___	___	___
6. galee	_____	___	___	___
7. tar	_____	___	___	___
8. chirost	_____	___	___	___
9. dalygub	_____	___	___	___
10. soume	_____	___	___	___

3 A woman is looking at a bird.

Listen and circle the word you hear.

WOMAN: That's an interesting _____ . The _____ are

1. (bird)/ bee   2. feathers / pheasants

dark. It definitely is not a _____ or a _____ .

3. duck / duckling   4. pelican / penguin

It has a very big _____ . Look! I can see its _____ in

5. bill / beak   6. crest / nest

that tree. It's very big too.

The bird is
a. a cockatoo.
b. a swan.
c. an eagle.
e. an owl.

4 Complete the sentences.

1. All birds have
   a. flippers.
   (b.) feathers.
   c. crests.

2. The _____ has very
   long legs.
   a. duck
   b. owl
   c. flamingo

3. The _____ has a very
   long neck.
   a. hawk
   b. swallow
   c. swan

4. The _____ has flippers.
   a. penguin
   b. hummingbird
   c. mouse

5. A butterfly is
   a. a bird.
   b. an insect.
   c. a rodent.

6. A _____ has black spots.
   a. swan
   b. spider
   c. ladybug

7. A _____ CAN'T fly.
   a. bee
   b. robin
   c. spider

8. A _____ does NOT have a
   long tail.
   a. mouse
   b. gull
   c. squirrel

5 Can you find:

1. an insect that rhymes with tree? _bee_

2. a rodent that rhymes with hat? _____

3. a part of a bird that rhymes with hill? _____

4. a bird that rhymes with towel? _____

5. a bird that rhymes with truck? _____

6. an insect that rhymes with dry? _____

7. a rodent that rhymes with house? _____

8. a part of a bird that rhymes with peak? _____

9. a part of a bird that rhymes with pail? _____

10. an insect that rhymes with ticket? _____

36 SPACE · THE MILITARY

1 Unscramble the words.

Put a check (√) in the correct column.

		Army	Air Force	Navy
1. lordsie	_soldier_	√	___	___
2. lipto	___	___	___	___
3. lefir	___	___	___	___
4. brebom	___	___	___	___
5. orlais	___	___	___	___
6. busnearim	___	___	___	___
7. labtetipsh	___	___	___	___
8. rapathuce	___	___	___	___
9. epej	___	___	___	___
10. nacnon	___	___	___	___

2 Cross out the word that does not belong.

1. Earth   Saturn   ~~Sun~~

2. marine   astronaut   soldier

3. space suit   fatigues   parachute

4. rifle   cannon   booster rocket

102

3 Read the sentences.

Look at photos 7–12 on page 77 in your PHOTO DICTIONARY and write True or False.

Correct the sentences that are false.

1. The man is on a star.

   False. He is on the moon.

2. He is a marine.

   _____

3. He is next to a flag.

   _____

4. The flag is red, white and blue.

   _____

5. The man is wearing fatigues.

   _____

6. There is a space ship to the right of the flag.

   _____

Now look at photos 8–9 on page 78.

7. These men are astronauts.

   _____

8. They are in the army.

   _____

9. They have a cannon.

   _____

4 Fill in the blanks with <u>in</u> or <u>on</u>.

1. The astronaut is *on* the moon.

2. He is _____ a space suit.

3. There are millions of stars _____ a galaxy.

4. We live _____ the planet Earth.

5. The astronauts are _____ the space shuttle.

6. The soldiers are _____ their fatigues.

7. They are _____ a jeep.

8. They are _____ a tank.

9. The radar antenna is _____ the battleship.

10. The helicopter is _____ the aircraft carrier.

**5 Listen to the conversations.
Circle the correct answer.**

1. What is the man's job?
   a. Astronaut.
   b. Soldier.
   c. Pilot.

2. What is the woman's job?
   a. Astronaut.
   b. Soldier.
   c. Pilot.

3. What is the man's job?
   a. Marine.
   b. Soldier.
   c. Sailor.

4. What is the man's job?
   a. Soldier.
   b. Astronaut.
   c. Pilot.

5. What is the man's job?
   a. Soldier.
   b. Sailor.
   c. Marine.

37 HOBBIES & GAMES SEWING & SUNDRIES

1 Match the words in column A with the pictures in column B.

	A		B
1.	_b_ Scrabble®	a.	
2.	_____ cards	b.	
3.	_____ Monopoly®	c.	
4.	_____ backgammon	d.	
5.	_____ checkers	e.	
6.	_____ chess	f.	

2 Unscramble the words.
Put a check (✓) in the correct column.

			Hobby	Craft	Game
1.	srnmatooy	_astronomy_	✓	___	___
2.	pulcisngt	_____	___	___	___
3.	tinkgint	_____	___	___	___
4.	darcs	_____	___	___	___
5.	thopphorayg	_____	___	___	___
6.	recksech	_____	___	___	___
7.	owodginkorw	_____	___	___	___

105

3 Complete the sentences.

1. You use a magnifying glass for
   a. astronomy.
   b. bird watching.
   c. stamp collecting. ⟵ (circled)

2. You use a loom for
   a. woodworking.
   b. weaving.
   c. knitting.

3. You use needles for
   a. knitting.
   b. painting.
   c. weaving.

4. You look at planets with a
   a. magnifying glass.
   b. protractor.
   c. telescope.

5. _____ is NOT a game.
   a. Scrabble®
   b. Chess
   c. Sewing

6. You draw a circle with a
   a. bow.
   b. compass.
   c. hook.

7. The needles, pins and scissors are in
   a. a pin cushion.
   b. an album.
   c. a sewing basket.

8. _____ does NOT use an album.
   a. Stamp collecting
   b. Photography
   c. Astronomy

4 There are six mistakes in the shopping list.

Circle the incorrect words.

Write the correct words below.

```
  ○   (pensils)      paint              string
      protractor     brush              ribbon
  ○   note book      mascing tape
      Kompess        sissors
      paper          loose-leaf binder
```

1. pencils

2. _____

3. _____

4. _____

5. _____

6. _____

106

5 **Listen to the conversations and circle the correct answer.**

1. What is the man doing?
   a. Stamp collecting.
   b. Bird watching.
   c. Coin collecting.

2. What is the man and woman's hobby?
   a. Stamp collecting.
   b. Coin collecting.
   c. Painting.

3. What are the man and woman doing?
   a. Playing Scrabble®.
   b. Playing chess.
   c. Playing Monopoly®.

4. What is the man's hobby?
   a. Bird watching.
   b. Astronomy.
   c. Sculpting.

5. What is the man doing?
   a. Knitting.
   b. Woodworking.
   c. Sculpting.

6. What are the man and woman playing?
   a. Chess.
   b. Monopoly®.
   c. Cards.

7. What is the woman going to do?
   a. Sew.
   b. Weave.
   c. Knit.

8. What is the woman's hobby?
   a. Photography.
   b. Astronomy.
   c. Painting.

6 **There are eight words in the box.**

Circle the words.

S	L	V	W	I	D	S	M	S	F
C	O	P	D	S	T	A	M	P	O
R	G	H	S	W	E	I	O	O	P
A	M	E	G	X	L	N	W	T	D
B	L	C	A	M	E	R	A	T	O
B	N	O	W	X	S	V	L	E	R
L	S	M	R	I	C	K	B	R	P
E	M	P	A	R	O	J	U	Y	O
P	R	A	I	E	P	S	M	U	S
L	A	S	N	F	E	U	C	H	S
N	T	S	T	R	I	N	G	O	M

LISTENING SCRIPT

1 NUMBERS • TIME

2 Listen and write the numbers.

1. My address is 25 East Fourth Street.
2. My zip code is 17642.
3. My phone number is 583-9924.
4. My area code is 719.
5. My social security number is 128-48-9823.

2 CALENDAR & HOLIDAYS • WEATHER & SEASONS

5 Listen to the weather forecast and circle the word you hear.

RADIO ANNOUNCER: Here's the weather forecast for tomorrow, January fifth. Tomorrow will be sunny and windy in the morning with temperatures around freezing. Thursday will also be very cold, the temperature dropping to below freezing.

3 SHAPES & MEASUREMENTS

2 A man wants to buy some curtains. Listen and circle the word you hear.

MAN: I'd like to buy some curtains for my living room windows.

SALESPERSON: Fine. Do you have the measurements?

MAN: Yes. The length is 10 feet, and the width is 5 feet.

4 MONEY & BANKING

4 A bank teller and a customer are talking. Listen and look at the bank slips. Put a check (√) next to the bank slip the customer is using.

TELLER: Good afternoon.

CUSTOMER: Good afternoon. I'd like to deposit $150.00 in my account.

TELLER: OK, but I need your account number on this slip.

CUSTOMER: Oh. It's 8-7-3-4-5-6-9.

TELLER: Thank you.

5 THE WORLD • THE UNITED STATES • CANADA

4 A woman is talking to a travel agent. Listen and circle the word you hear.

AGENT: Fine. Where would you like to go for your vacation?

WOMAN: I'm not sure. Maybe to China. Is a trip there very expensive?

AGENT: Yes. But we have a very interesting trip to Australia.

WOMAN: Hmmm. I don't think I want to go there. How about Russia?

AGENT: That's very expensive too. Maybe you'd enjoy a trip to Europe.

WOMAN: I went there last year.

AGENT: Oh. How about South America? We have a special trip to Brazil. It's interesting and not very expensive.

WOMAN: That sounds great!

6 THE CITY

4 A woman is asking for directions. Listen and circle the word you hear.

WOMAN: Excuse me. Is there a newsstand near here?

MAN: Yes. Walk two or three blocks. You'll see a bus stop on the corner. Turn right and walk another block. There's a subway entrance in front of a new office building. Go inside and you'll find it there.

WOMAN: Thanks a lot.

7 THE SUPERMARKET • FRUIT • VEGETABLES

2 Juan and María are talking about dinner. Listen and circle the word you hear.

MARÍA: Let's make macaroni and cheese for dinner.

JUAN: Good idea! And we can have a salad too.

MARÍA: OK. What do we need?

JUAN: Well, we have milk, but we need some cheese.

MARÍA: What about butter?

JUAN: We don't have any. We need to buy some. And we have lettuce for the salad, but we need some tomatoes and cucumbers.

MARÍA: What do you want to drink?

108

JUAN: Orange juice. Do we have any?
MARÍA: No. We need some. What about dessert?
JUAN: Let's buy some raspberries. Oh, and let's buy some bread too.
MARÍA: Great. Let's go to the supermarket now.

8 THE MENU • FAST FOODS & SNACKS

4 A customer is ordering a meal at Daphne's Diner. Listen and circle the word you hear.

WAITER: Are you ready to order?
CUSTOMER: Yes. First I'd like some tomato soup. Then I'd like the roast chicken.
WAITER: Would you like any vegetables?
CUSTOMER: Carrots, please.
WAITER: OK. Something to drink?
CUSTOMER: A cup of tea.
WAITER: Dessert?
CUSTOMER: Yes. I'd like some apple pie.
WAITER: Anything else?
CUSTOMER: No, that's all, thanks.

9 THE POST OFFICE • THE OFFICE

2 A postal clerk and a customer are talking. Listen and look at the pictures. What is the man sending? Put a check (√) next to the correct picture.

MAN: I want to mail this letter to my friend in Chicago. It's very important.
CLERK: Do you want to send it express mail?
MAN: No, but I want to know when my friend receives the letter.
CLERK: Then send it certified mail. When your friend gets your letter, we mail you a return receipt.
MAN: That sounds good. Thank you.

10 OCCUPATIONS

4 Listen to the conversations. Circle the correct answers.

ANNOUNCER: Number 1.
WOMAN: What color do you want your kitchen?
MAN: Yellow.
WOMAN: OK. I'll start work tomorrow.
ANNOUNCER: What is the woman's occupation?

ANNOUNCER: Number 2.
MAN: OK, class. For homework read from page 40 to page 60 in your books.
WOMAN: Are we going to have a test?
MAN: You'll have a test next Friday.
ANNOUNCER: What is the man's occupation?

ANNOUNCER: Number 3.
WOMAN: I'd like a hamburger and french fries, please.
MAN: Anything to drink?
WOMAN: A Coke, please.
ANNOUNCER: What is the man's occupation?

ANNOUNCER: Number 4.
WOMAN: How would you like your hundred dollars, sir?

MAN: In tens, please.
WOMAN: Ten, twenty, thirty, forty, fifty, sixty, seventy, eighty, ninety, one hundred. One hundred dollars.
MAN: Thank you.
ANNOUNCER: What is the woman's occupation?

ANNOUNCER: Number 5.
WOMAN: These are beautiful flowers. How much are they?
MAN: They're $5.00.
ANNOUNCER: What is the man's occupation?

ANNOUNCER: Number 6.
MAN: And now the international report with Yolanda Davis.
WOMAN: Thank you, John. Today in France, the franc fell to a record low. In England the pound remained stable. More on Wall Street's reaction after this word from our local sponsor.
ANNOUNCER: What is the woman's occupation?

ANNOUNCER: Number 7.
MAN: Does anything hurt?
WOMAN: Yes. My front tooth.
MAN: Let's see. Now open your mouth wide.
ANNOUNCER: What is the man's occupation?

ANNOUNCER: Number 8.
(telephone ring)
WOMAN: Mr. Lee's office.
MAN: May I speak to Mr. Lee, please?
WOMAN: I'm sorry. He's not in. Can I take a message?
MAN: Thanks. I'll call back tomorrow.
ANNOUNCER: What is the woman's occupation?

11 THE BODY • COSMETICS & TOILETRIES

6 A salesclerk is putting makeup on a woman. Listen and circle the word you hear.

CLERK: OK. I finished putting the base on your face. Now here's a little blush for your cheeks. What would you like on your eyes?
WOMAN: A little eyeliner and some mascara.
CLERK: What about eye shadow?
WOMAN: No thanks.
CLERK: Fine. Would you like anything else?
WOMAN: Just lipstick, please.

12 ACTION AT HOME • ACTION AT THE GYM • ACTION AT SCHOOL

5 Marsha Rifkin is talking about a typical morning. Listen and match the times in column A with the actions in column B.

MARSHA: I get up at 5:30 every day. At 6:00 I bend and stretch. I eat breakfast at 6:30. At 7:00 I take a shower. Then at 7:30 I watch TV. (I like to watch the news.) I always drink a cup of coffee at 8:00, and at 8:30 I leave for work.

13 THE DOCTOR • THE DENTIST

3 A doctor is talking to her 10-year-old patient Jimmy. Listen and complete the chart.

DOCTOR: Well, Jimmy, what seems to be the problem?
JIMMY: I have a bad cold. (sound of coughing)
DOCTOR: And you also have a cough.
JIMMY: Yes. And I have a headache too.
DOCTOR: Put this thermometer under your tongue. That's right. Now, I'm going to listen to your heart and lungs with my stethoscope. Uh-huh. Very good. Let's look at the thermometer now.—You don't have a fever. Here's some aspirin for your headache. And here's a prescription for some cough medicine.
JIMMY: Thank you.

14 THE FAMILY

4 Carol and Eric are having a dinner party. Listen and look at the guest list. Put a check (√) next to the people they are going to invite.

CAROL: Let's see. We can have six people for dinner.
ERIC: Well, there's Mother and Father.
CAROL: That's two people. What about Aunt Rosa?
ERIC: She has a cold. She can't come. But Aunt Hilda can come.
CAROL: And Uncle Herb?
ERIC: No, he's in California. We can't invite him. Uncle Sam is here. I'm sure he can come. Now we have four people. We can invite two more.
CAROL: OK. What about Cousin Ellie?
ERIC: Cousins Ellie and Rhoda are in Texas. But we can invite Cousins Frank and Irene.
CAROL: Great! Now we have six.

15 EMOTIONS • OPPOSITES

2 Listen to the people. How do they feel? Choose the correct words from the box.

ANNOUNCER: Number 1.
MAN: (laughing) This is great!

ANNOUNCER: Number 2.
WOMAN: (angrily) I told you to never do that again.

ANNOUNCER: Number 3.
MAN: (in frightened voice) Did you hear that?

ANNOUNCER: Number 4.
WOMAN: (yawning and bored) Ho hum. What can we do now?

ANNOUNCER: Number 5.
MAN: (confused) Huh? I don't understand. What do you mean?

ANNOUNCER: Number 6.
WOMAN: (determined) I'll definitely be there at noon.

ANNOUNCER: Number 7.
MAN: (surprised) What!? You're kidding!

16 MEN'S WEAR • WOMEN'S WEAR • MEN'S & WOMEN'S WEAR • ACCESSORIES

4 A woman wants to buy a sweater. Listen and look at the pictures. Put a check (√) next to the sweater the customer wants to buy.

CLERK: Can I help you?
WOMAN: Yes. I'd like to buy a sweater.
CLERK: These are very nice.
WOMAN: Yes, but those are solid. I want one with a pattern.
CLERK: Striped or plaid?
WOMAN: That striped one is pretty. What colors does it come in?
CLERK: Black and white or gray and white.
WOMAN: I like the gray and white.
CLERK: The gray and white comes with a crewneck or turtleneck.
WOMAN: I'll take the crewneck, please.

17 HOUSING • BACKYARD & GARDEN

5 A woman is showing her new apartment to a friend. Listen and look at the pictures. Put a check (√) next to the correct floor plan.

WOMAN A: Hi! Come on in.
WOMAN B: Hi!
WOMAN A: So, this is my new apartment!
WOMAN B: Oh, it's beautiful!
WOMAN A: Well, this is the living room . . .
WOMAN B: It's very light.
WOMAN A: Yes. There are four windows. And here's the kitchen.
WOMAN B: Oh, there's a window in the kitchen too.
WOMAN A: Yes.
WOMAN B: And how many bedrooms are there?
WOMAN A: There are two bedrooms. And there are two bathrooms too.
WOMAN B: It's a nice apartment.
WOMAN A: Thanks. I like it too.

18 THE LIVING ROOM • THE DINING ROOM

4 A mother is telling her son how to set the table. Listen and circle the word you hear.

MOTHER: Put the napkin on the plate.
SON: Where do the forks go?
MOTHER: Put the dinner fork to the left of the plate. And put the salad fork to the left of the dinner fork.
SON: What about the water glass?
MOTHER: Put it to the right of the cup.
SON: And the knife?
MOTHER: Put it to the right of the dinner plate. And put the teaspoon to the right of the soupspoon. And that's it!

19 THE BEDROOM • THE BATHROOM

5 Listen to the conversations. Are the people in the bedroom or in the bathroom? Put a check (√) in the correct column.

ANNOUNCER: Number 1.
MAN: Where's the light switch?
WOMAN: It's above the chest of drawers.

ANNOUNCER: Number 2.
WOMAN: Is there any more soap?
MAN: Yes. There's some in the soap dispenser.

ANNOUNCER: Number 3.
MAN: Which is the hot water faucet?
WOMAN: It's on the left.

ANNOUNCER: Number 4.
WOMAN: I'm really cold.
MAN: Well, turn on the electric blanket.

ANNOUNCER: Number 5.
MAN: Where's my book?
WOMAN: It's here on the night table.

ANNOUNCER: Number 6.
WOMAN: Which towel can I use?
MAN: The guest towels are to the right of the sink.

ANNOUNCER: Number 7.
MAN: Here's a pillowcase.
WOMAN: And here are two sheets.

ANNOUNCER: Number 8.
WOMAN: Where are my jeans?
MAN: They're in the dresser.

ANNOUNCER: Number 9.
MAN: The aspirin isn't in the medicine cabinet.
WOMAN: I know. It's on the shelf above the towel rack.

ANNOUNCER: Number 10.
WOMAN: Good night. I'm turning off the lamp.
MAN: OK. Good night.

20 THE KITCHEN • KITCHENWARE

5 Lisa and Irving are making breakfast. Listen and circle the word you hear.

LISA: Where's the coffee pot?
IRVING: I don't have one. I have a coffee maker. It's on the counter next to the sink.
LISA: OK. And where's the toaster?
IRVING: To the right of the stove. Anything else?
LISA: Bread.
IRVING: Oh, it's in the refrigerator. And I'll get the cups.
LISA: Good. And don't forget the plates.

21 THE NURSERY • THE PLAYGROUND

4 Listen to the conversations. Are the people in the nursery or at the playground? Put a check (√) in the correct column.

ANNOUNCER: Number 1.
WOMAN: Take your pail and shovel and go play in the sandbox.
CHILD: OK.

ANNOUNCER: Number 2.
MAN: Where's the baby bottle?
WOMAN: It's to the left of the food warmer.

ANNOUNCER: Number 3.
CHILD: Where's Mommy?
CHILD: She's sitting on the bench.

ANNOUNCER: Number 4.
CHILD: Come and play on the jungle gym.
CHILD: OK. I'll be right there.

ANNOUNCER: Number 5.
WOMAN: What's Molly doing?
MAN: She's sitting on the rug and playing with her stuffed animals.

ANNOUNCER: Number 6.
WOMAN: Look at those beautiful kites!
CHILD: Oh! Can I have one too?

ANNOUNCER: Number 7.
WOMAN: Where's the baby?
MAN: He's sleeping in his crib.

ANNOUNCER: Number 8.
CHILD: I'm thirsty.
MAN: Well, there's a water fountain over there.

ANNOUNCER: Number 9.
CHILD: See-saw, Margery Daw.
WOMAN: Come on, Tommy. Get off the see-saw. It's time to go home!

ANNOUNCER: Number 10.
MAN: Sit on the swing and I'll push you.
CHILD: No. I want to go on the slide!

22 THE LAUNDRY ROOM • TOOLS • CONSTRUCTION

5 A salesperson and a customer are talking. Listen and circle the word you hear.

SALESPERSON: Can I help you?
CUSTOMER: Yes. I need a saw and an electric drill, please.
SALESPERSON: OK. Anything else?
CUSTOMER: Yes. Some screws and a paintbrush.
SALESPERSON: Do you need paint too?
CUSTOMER: No. I have a can.
SALESPERSON: Anything else?
CUSTOMER: No, that's all, thanks.

23 ELECTRONICS

4 Listen to the sounds. Which machines make them? Choose a machine from the words in the box.

ANNOUNCER: Number 1.
(sound of push button phone being dialed. Followed by either busy signal or normal ring)

ANNOUNCER: Number 2.
(sound of typing on electronic typewriter—2 lines so that bell indicating page end is heard twice)

ANNOUNCER: Number 3.
(someone turning dial on radio, so you can hear all the stations)

ANNOUNCER: Number 4.
(record playing with needle skipping)

ANNOUNCER: Number 5.
　　　　　　(answering machine message with beep heard at end)
WOMAN: Hello. This is Sharon Rotell. I'm sorry I can't answer your call. Please leave your name and phone number, and I'll get back to you. Wait for the beep. BEEP

ANNOUNCER: Number 6.
　　　　　　(TV program—soap opera)

ANNOUNCER: Number 7.
　　　　　　(sound of clicking camera and winding of film)

24　LAND & WATER

5 Listen to this radio commercial. Put a check (√) next to the correct travel poster.

ANNOUNCER: This spring come to beautiful Switzerland. Climb to the wonderful mountain peaks. Walk in the beautiful meadows filled with flowers of all colors. Yes. Come to Switzerland this spring. For more information, call The Swiss Tourist Agency at 543-9876. That's 543-9876.

25　THE CAR

4 A woman is talking to a police officer. Which car did the woman see? Put a check (√) next to the correct car.

POLICE OFFICER: Did you see the car?
WOMAN: Yes. It was gray.
POLICE OFFICER: What kind of car? A station wagon? A convertible . . . ?
WOMAN: No, it was a sedan.
POLICE OFFICER: Did you see the license plate?
WOMAN: Yes. The license plate number was 8839.
POLICE OFFICER: 8839?
WOMAN: Yes, that's right.

26　THE TRAIN, BUS & TAXI

4 A man is talking to an agent at an information booth. Listen and circle the word you hear.

MAN: Is that clock correct?
AGENT: Yes. It's 4:30.
MAN: What time does the train to Philadelphia leave?
AGENT: At 5:00.
MAN: And where can I get a ticket?
AGENT: At the counter over there.
MAN: I see. And what is the track number?
AGENT: Look at the departure board for that information, please.
MAN: OK. And can I have a schedule?
AGENT: Here you are.
MAN: Thank you very much.

27　ROUTES & ROAD SIGNS

3 A woman is talking to a police officer. Listen and look at the map. Where is the post office? Put a check (√) next to the correct number.

WOMAN: Excuse me. Where's the post office?
OFFICER: Drive to the intersection. There's a traffic light there. Turn right at the intersection. Then turn left at the stop sign. The post office is on the first corner to your left.
WOMAN: Thank you.

28　THE AIRPORT

5 A passenger is talking to a ticket agent at the airport. Listen and look at the seating plan. Put a check (√) next to the passenger's boarding pass.

AGENT: Can I help you?
PASSENGER: Yes. I'd like a ticket to Miami.
AGENT: For the 9:00 plane?
PASSENGER: No, the 10:00 plane, please.
AGENT: OK. Would you like a window or an aisle seat?
PASSENGER: An aisle seat.
AGENT: OK. here you are. That's gate 7A.
PASSENGER: Thank you.

29　THE WATERFRONT ● THE BEACH

4 Are the people at the waterfront or at the beach? Listen and put a check (√) in the correct column.

NARRATOR: Number 1.
MAN: Where's the ferry?
WOMAN: The ferry? It's at pier 7.

NARRATOR: Number 2.
MAN: Is the cargo all here?
MAN: Yes. It's all on the ship.

NARRATOR: Number 3.
BOY: What's that?
WOMAN: It's a tugboat.

NARRATOR: Number 4.
MAN: Is this the bow or the stern?
WOMAN: It's the stern.

NARRATOR: Number 5.
BOY: What a beautiful sand castle!
GIRL: I made it with my pail and shovel.

NARRATOR: Number 6.
BOY: What are you doing?
GIRL: Looking for shells.

NARRATOR: Number 7.
MAN: What time is it?
WOMAN: I don't know. Why don't you ask one of the dock workers?

NARRATOR: Number 8.
BOY: What's that?
GIRL: It's a buoy.

30　WATER SPORTS ● WINTER SPORTS

5 Listen and circle the correct sport.

ANNOUNCER: Number 1.
WOMAN: The surf is really high today.
MAN: Yes. Let's get our surfboards.

ANNOUNCER: Number 2.
MAN: Do you have your mask?
WOMAN: Yes. And my air tank is full.

ANNOUNCER: Number 3.
WOMAN: Here's your life jacket.
MAN: Thanks. Now let's get onto the raft.

ANNOUNCER: Number 4.
WOMAN: Would you like me to row now?
MAN: OK. Here are the oars.

ANNOUNCER: Number 5.
WOMAN: Is the motorboat ready?
MAN: Yes. Get your water skis.

ANNOUNCER: Number 6.
MAN: Now sit on the sled.
GIRL: OK. I'm on the sled.

31 SPECTATOR SPORTS • OTHER SPORTS

5 Listen and circle the correct sport.

ANNOUNCER: Number 1.
MAN: And the batter is nearing home plate. The third baseman throws the ball to the catcher. The catcher tags the runner. And—he's out!

ANNOUNCER: Number 2.
(sound of ping pong ball being hit back and forth across table)

ANNOUNCER: Number 3.
MAN: Who's number 11?
WOMAN: He's the quarterback.
MAN: And who's number 23?
WOMAN: The halfback.

ANNOUNCER: Number 4.
(sound of tennis ball being hit back and forth across court)
MAN: The score is 15–love.

ANNOUNCER: Number 5.
MAN: Let's put up our tent under that tree.
WOMAN: OK. And we can put the camper over here.

ANNOUNCER: Number 6.
GIRL: This bowling ball is very heavy.
BOY: But you knocked down 8 pins!

ANNOUNCER: Number 7.
WOMAN: (a little out of breath) Do you jog every day?
MAN: (also a little out of breath) No, only on weekends.

ANNOUNCER: Number 8.
MAN: Now you put the arrow across the bow— like this. And then you aim for the target!

ANNOUNCER: Number 9.
WOMAN: Is the horse ready?
MAN: No. The saddle isn't on.

ANNOUNCER: Number 10.
MAN: He's very good.
WOMAN: Yes. He has a black belt.

32 ENTERTAINMENT • MUSICAL INSTRUMENTS

4 What do you hear? Listen and circle the correct answer.

ANNOUNCER: Number 1.
(orchestral music)

ANNOUNCER: Number 2.
(rock singer)

ANNOUNCER: Number 3.
(choral music)

ANNOUNCER: Number 4.
(operatic aria—from Carmen)

ANNOUNCER: Number 5.
(male singing—not opera)

ANNOUNCER: Number 6.
(sounds of audience applauding, shouts of "Bravo!")

ANNOUNCER: Number 7.
(actor reciting Hamlet's soliloquy)

ANNOUNCER: Number 8.
(piano sonata)

ANNOUNCER: Number 9.
(drum roll)

ANNOUNCER: Number 10.
(flute)

33 THE ZOO & PETS

6 Listen to the sounds. What animals make them? Circle the correct answer.

ANNOUNCER: Number 1.
(lion's roar)

ANNOUNCER: Number 2.
(snake's hiss)

ANNOUNCER: Number 3.
(dog barking)

ANNOUNCER: Number 4.
(parrot talking)

ANNOUNCER: Number 5.
(bear growling)

ANNOUNCER: Number 6.
(cat meowing)

ANNOUNCER: Number 7.
(parakeet chirping)

34 THE FARM • FISH & SEA ANIMALS

5 Listen to the sounds. Which animals make them? Circle the correct answer.

ANNOUNCER: Number 1.
(sound of pig)

ANNOUNCER: Number 2.
(sound of chicken)

ANNOUNCER: Number 3.
(sound of horse)

ANNOUNCER: Number 4.
(sound of cow)

ANNOUNCER: Number 5.
(sound of lamb)

ANNOUNCER: Number 6.
(sound of rooster)

35 BIRDS • INSECTS & RODENTS

3 A woman is looking at a bird. Listen and circle the word you hear.

WOMAN: That's an interesting bird. The feathers are dark. It definitely is not a duck or a pelican. It has a very big beak. Look! I can see its nest in that tree. It's very big too.

36 SPACE • THE MILITARY

5 Listen to these conversations. Circle the correct answer.

ANNOUNCER: Number 1.
MAN: I get up early every day, put on my fatigues and drive my jeep.
ANNOUNCER: What is the man's job?

ANNOUNCER: Number 2.
WOMAN: I love being in space. The Earth looks beautiful from the space shuttle.
ANNOUNCER: What is the woman's job?

ANNOUNCER: Number 3.
MAN: My job is a little like a sailor's. But I'm not in the Navy. I work on the land and on the sea.
ANNOUNCER: What is the man's job?

ANNOUNCER: Number 4.
MAN: I fly all day. Sometimes I fly a helicopter. Sometimes I fly a fighter plane.
ANNOUNCER: What is the man's job?

ANNOUNCER: Number 5.
MAN: Last month I was on a submarine for ten days. This month I'm working on a battleship.
ANNOUNCER: What is the man's job?

37 HOBBIES & GAMES • SEWING & SUNDRIES

5 Listen to the conversations and circle the correct answer.

ANNOUNCER: Number 1.
MAN: Look at that eagle!
WOMAN: That isn't an eagle. It's a hawk.
ANNOUNCER: What is the man doing?

ANNOUNCER: Number 2.
WOMAN: Here's a 1975 silver dollar.
MAN: And here's a penny from 1917.
ANNOUNCER: What is the man and woman's hobby?

ANNOUNCER: Number 3.
WOMAN: W-I-N-D-O-W. Window.
MAN: That's four, five, six, eight, nine, thirteen. Doubled—that's twenty-six points.
ANNOUNCER: What are the man and woman doing?

ANNOUNCER: Number 4.
MAN: Look. I can see Saturn!
WOMAN: Can I look too?
ANNOUNCER: What is the man's hobby?

ANNOUNCER: Number 5.
MAN: Knit one, purl two. Knit one, purl two.
WOMAN: What are you making?
MAN: A sweater.
ANNOUNCER: What is the man doing?

ANNOUNCER: Number 6.
MAN: Who deals?
WOMAN: It's my deal. (sound of cards being shuffled)
ANNOUNCER: What are the man and woman playing?

ANNOUNCER: Number 7.
WOMAN: My button fell off.
MAN: That's OK. I have a needle and thread.
ANNOUNCER: What is the woman going to do?

ANNOUNCER: Number 8.
WOMAN: OK. I'm going to take your picture now. Say "cheese."
MAN: Cheese!
ANNOUNCER: What is the woman's hobby?

ANSWER KEY

1 NUMBERS • TIME

1
2. h
3. b
4. e
5. j
6. c

7. g
8. f
9. a
10. i

2
1. 25, 4
2. 17642
3. 583-9924

4. 719
5. 128-48-9823

4 Wrong answers are 4 and 8.

The student's grade is 70%.

5
1. Vilma lives in the third apartment.
2. Cathy lives in the first apartment.
3. Bill lives in the second apartment.
4. Tom lives in the fourth apartment.

6
2. ten to five
3. seven to four
4. eight thirty

5. two o'clock
6. one in the morning

2 CALENDAR & HOLIDAYS • WEATHER & SEASONS

1
6 June
3 March
5 May
11 November
2 February
9 September

4 April
10 October
8 August
1 January
12 December
7 July

2
2. False. There is one holiday in March.
3. False. Mother's Day is in May. Father's Day is in June.
4. True

3
2. cool
3. freezing
4. warm

5. cold
6. below freezing

4
2. Sunday
3. sunny
4. windy

5. Monday
6. spring

5
2. January
3. sunny
4. windy
5. freezing

6. Thursday
7. cold
8. freezing

3 SHAPES & MEASUREMENTS

1
2. a
3. e
4. c

5. f
6. b

2
1. measurements
2. length
3. feet

4. width
5. 5

3
2. True.
3. False. It's a right triangle.
4. False. The width is 2 inches.
5. True
6. True

4 These shapes are in the picture: triangle, spiral, square, parallel lines.

4 MONEY & BANKING

1
2. d
3. b

4. e
5. a

2
2. c
3. a

4. b
5. e

3
2. Fifty
3. 14.00

4. Four hundred sixty-nine
5. 18.00

4 The customer is using slip 1.

5
2. a
3. c

4. c
5. b

5 THE WORLD • THE UNITED STATES • CANADA

1 2. It's in Africa.
    3. It's in Asia.
    4. It's in North America.
    5. It's in Asia.
    6. It's in Europe.

2 2. False. Illinois is west of Indiana.
    3. False. Quebec is east of Ontario.
    4. False. Rhode Island is south of Massachusetts.

3
Colombia	Argentina
Ecuador	Bolivia
Peru	Brazil
Chile	Chile
Argentina	Colombia
Bolivia	Ecuador
Falkland Islands	Falkland Islands
Paraguay	French Guiana
Uruguay	Guyana
Brazil	Paraguay
French Guiana	Peru
Suriname	Suriname
Guyana	Uruguay
Venezuela	Venezuela

4 2. Australia
    3. Russia
    4. Europe
    5. South America
    6. Brazil

6 THE CITY

1 2. There is a flag on 11th Street. There isn't a flag on 10th Street.
    3. There is a traffic light on 10th Street. There is a stop sign on 11th Street.
    4. There is a phone booth on 10th Street. There isn't a phone booth on 11th Street.
    5. There is a bus stop on 11th Street. There isn't a bus stop on 10th Street.
    6. There is a newsstand on 11th Street. There isn't a newsstand on 10th Street.

3 2. e
    3. a
    4. f
    5. b
    6. c

4 2. bus stop
    3. corner
    4. subway
    5. office building
The woman probably wants a newspaper.

7 THE SUPERMARKET • FRUIT • VEGETABLES

1 2. bacon (Meats and Poultry)
    3. soup (Canned Goods)
    4. macaroni (Packaged Goods)
    5. milk (Dairy)
    6. frozen dinner (Frozen Foods)
    7. chicken (Meats and Poultry)
    8. yogurt (Dairy)

2 2. milk
    3. cheese
    4. butter
    5. lettuce
    6. tomatoes
    7. cucumbers
    8. orange
    9. raspberries
    10. bread

3
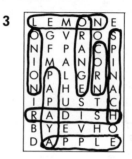

Fruits: lemon, apple, papaya
Vegetables: radish, corn, spinach, onion

8 THE MENU • FAST FOODS & SNACKS

1 2. True
    3. True
    4. False. There are three kinds of soup.
    5. I don't know.
    6. False. Stuffed tomatoes is an entrée.

2 You can order meal 3, 4 or 6.

4 2. roast
    3. carrots
    4. tea
    5. apple pie

tomato soup	.75
roast chicken	7.85
carrots	.95
tea	.50
apple pie	1.50
Total	$11.55

9 THE POST OFFICE • THE OFFICE

1 2. False. The return address is 20 West 68th Street.
    3. False. Miriam's zip code is 90403.
    4. True
    5. False. The envelope is a rectangle.

2 The man is sending a certified letter (picture 3).

3 You usually don't find these things on a desk: secretary, wastepaper basket, file cabinet, bulletin board.

4 2. stationery
    3. envelope
    4. pencil holder
    5. typewriter

10 OCCUPATIONS

1 2. f   5. g
   3. a   6. c
   4. b   7. e

2 2. journalist   4. secretary
   3. waiter, waitress   5. teacher

3 *inside:* teller, optometrist, butcher
   Outside: construction worker, bricklayer, window
   washer, sanitation worker

4 2. c   6. b
   3. c   7. a
   4. b   8. c
   5. c

11 THE BODY • COSMETICS & TOILETRIES

1 2. neck   9. stomach
   3. shoulder   10. thigh
   4. elbow   11. knee
   5. wrist   12. calf
   6. thumb   13. ankle
   7. waist   14. foot
   8. hip   15. toe

2 2. lip (Head)   5. shoulder (Arm)
   3. palm (Hand)   6. temple (Head)
   4. shin (Leg)   7. thumb (Hand)

3 2. leg   4. elbow
   3. ankle   5. beard

4 2. g   5. b
   3. a   6. d
   4. f   7. e

5 2. b
   3. a
   4. b

6 2. face   5. mascara
   3. blush   6. eye shadow
   4. eyeliner   7. lipstick

The woman looks like picture 2.

12 ACTION AT HOME • ACTION AT THE GYM • ACTION AT SCHOOL

1 2. d   6. c
   3. g   7. e
   4. i   8. a
   5. h   9. b

2 2. gets up   5. brushes his teeth
   3. takes a shower   6. shaves
   4. dries off   7. gets dressed

4 2. False. She's taking   4. True
   a bath.   5. False. She's washing
   3. False. She's brushing   her face.
   her hair.   6. True

5 2. e   5. g
   3. d   6. c
   4. a   7. b

6 2. a   4. e
   3. b   5. c

13 THE DOCTOR • THE DENTIST

1 2. a   headache   4. e   scratch
   3. b   overbite   5. d   stomachache

2 2. c   5. a
   3. c   6. c
   4. b

3 b. No   g. Yes
   c. Yes   h. No
   d. Yes   i. No
   e. No   j. Yes
   f. No

4 You usually don't find these things in a medicine cabinet: stethoscope, scale, x-ray, Novocain.

5 2. False. She's a doctor. 5. False. She's 57 years
   3. True   old.
   4. I don't know.   6. True

14 THE FAMILY

1 2. son   8. aunt
   3. uncle   9. sister
   4. mother   10. daughter
   5. niece   11. brother
   6. father   12. husband
   7. nephew

2 2. mother   8. uncle
   3. niece   9. father
   4. aunt   10. nephew
   5. sister   11. brother
   6. daughter   12. husband

3 2. brother   7. uncle
   3. Richard   8. daughter
   4. son-in-law   9. cousins
   5. sister-in-law   10. children,
   6. brothers   grandchildren

4 Carol and Eric are going to invite: Mother, Father,
   Aunt Hilda, Uncle Sam, Cousin Frank and Cousin
   Irene.

5 2. brother
   3. sister-in-law
   4. daughter

15 EMOTIONS • OPPOSITES

1
2. b
3. b
4. b

2
2. furious
3. scared
4. bored
5. confused
6. determined
7. surprised

3
2. f
3. a
4. c
5. d
6. j
7. b
8. e
9. h
10. i

4
2. False. She looks happy.
3. False. It's straight.
4. True
5. True
6. False. It's heavy.

5
2. Joan, Anne, sad
3. is short, curly
4. tight, dress is
5. is , is light
6. wide, belt is narrow

---

16 MEN'S WEAR • WOMEN'S WEAR • MEN & WOMEN'S WEAR • ACCESSORIES

1
2. For Men
3. For Men & Women
4. For Women
5. For Men & Women
6. For Women
7. For Men & Women
8. For Men & Women
9. For Women
10. For Men & Women
11. For Women
12. For Men

2
2. green
3. red
4. black
5. purple
6. white
7. gray

3
2. True
3. True
4. False. There are nightgowns and slips in the lingerie department.
5. True

4 The customer wants to buy sweater 3.

5

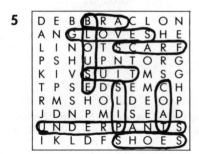

6
2. plaid
3. pearls
4. gold
5. scarf
6. robe

17 HOUSING • BACKYARD & GARDEN

1
2. True
3. True
4. True
5. I don't know.
6. False. There are two closets in the living room.

2
2. closet
3. lawn
4. leaf
5. barbecue
6. antenna

3
2. daisy
3. tulip
4. geranium
5. azalea
6. pansy
7. snapdragon
8. daffodil

4
1. azalea
2. daffodil
3. daisy
4. geranium
5. pansy
6. rose
7. snapdragon
8. tulip

5 Floor plan 2 is the woman's apartment.

6
2. b
3. a
4. b
5. c
6. a

---

18 THE LIVING ROOM • THE DINING ROOM

1
2. f fireplace
3. a centerpiece
4. d armchair
5. b soupspoon
6. e sideboard

2
2. couch (Living Room)
3. ottoman (Living Room)
4. sideboard (Dining Room)
5. fireplace (Living Room)
6. napkin (Dining Room)
7. bookcase (Living Room)

3 *Possible answers:*
2. On table A the cup is on a saucer. On table B there is no saucer.
3. On table A there are three flowers in the vase. On table B there are four.
4. On table B there is a soupspoon. On table A there is no soupspoon.
5. On table A the water glass is to the right of the wine glass. On table B the water glass is to the left of the wine glass.
6. On table A the wine and water glasses are to the right of the plate. On table B they are to the left.
7. On table A the water glass is full. On table B it is empty.
8. On table A the forks are to the left of the napkin. On table B the dinner fork is on the napkin.

4
2. plate
3. forks
4. dinner
5. salad
6. water
7. cup
8. knife
9. teaspoon
10. soupspoon

5

3 1. bowl, measuring cup, measuring spoons, egg beater
   2. measuring cup, rolling pin, measuring spoons, knife, peeler

4 2. dish towel   5. spatula
   3. roaster   6. ladle
   4. grater

5 2. maker   6. stove
   3. counter   7. refrigerator
   4. sink   8. cups
   5. toaster   9. plates

19 THE BEDROOM • THE BATHROOM

1 2. g bathtub   6. b toothbrush
   3. h doorknob   7. d headboard
   4. a nightstand   8. e bedspread
   5. c washcloth

2 2. False. The bath towel is on the bathtub.
   3. True
   4. False. There is soap in the soap dispenser.
   5. True
   6. False. The hot water faucet isn't on.
   7. False. There are two toothbrushes in the toothbrush holder.

3 2. b   6. c
   3. a   7. b
   4. b   8. a
   5. c

4 2. drawers   5. chest (of drawers)
   3. mirror   6. carpet, rug
   4. bedspread   7. dust ruffle

5 2. Bathroom   7. Bedroom
   3. Bathroom   8. Bedroom
   4. Bedroom   9. Bathroom
   5. Bedroom   10. Bedroom
   6. Bathroom

20 THE KITCHEN • KITCHENWARE

1 2. g   6. h
   3. a   7. f
   4. e   8. d
   5. b

2

```
A S T R A I N E R R
L T H O P M O R O A
M R I P O T S R J A
I A I B O W L S I T
X V N N T S P B I E
E E S I C I R E N R
X L A B O P A R E R
R O F M C H B R T
```

21 THE NURSERY • THE PLAYGROUND

1 2. Nursery   7. Playground
   3. Playground   8. Playground
   4. Playground   9. Playground
   5. Nursery   10. Nursery
   6. Nursery

2 2. carriage   4. doll carriage
   3. tricycle   5. skateboard

3 2. in   6. in
   3. on   7. on
   4. in   8. on
   5. on

4 2. Nursery   7. Nursery
   3. Playground   8. Playground
   4. Playground   9. Playground
   5. Nursery   10. Playground
   6. Playground

22 THE LAUNDRY ROOM • TOOLS • CONSTRUCTION

1 2. a   5. d
   3. f   6. e
   4. b

2 2. f clothesline   5. b sandpaper
   3. g paintbrush   6. d workbench
   4. a screwdriver   7. c backhoe

3 2. c, d   4. a, c, d
   3. b, d   5. c, e

4 2. open   5. white
   3. washer   6. in front of
   4. laundry basket   7. to the right of

5 2. an electric   4. paintbrush
   3. screws   5. can

The woman is going to build and paint a desk (c).

23 ELECTRONICS

1   4, 6, 7, 9

2

3   2. screen   6. battery
      3. headphone   7. tape recorder
      4. keyboard   8. slide projector
      5. camera

4   2. typewriter   5. answering machine
      3. radio   6. TV
      4. record player   7. camera

---

24 LAND AND WATER

1   2. tree (Land)   5. lake (Water)
      3. pond (Water)   6. river (Water)
      4. dune (Land)

2   2. mountain, hill   4. forest
      3. lake, river   5. pond, lake

3   2. dry   6. dark
      3. desert   7. high
      4. hard   8. low
      5. brook

4   2. True
      3. False. There is a hill behind the meadow.
      4. False. There is a pond to the left of the trees.

5   Poster 2

---

25 THE CAR

1   2. taillight   9. gas pedal
      3. bumper   10. gearshift
      4. trunk   11. seat
      5. tire   12. steering wheel
      6. hubcap   13. turn signal
      7. clutch   14. speedometer
      8. brake   15. windshield wiper

2   2. True   4. False. It's a sedan.
      3. False. The car is old. 5. True

3   2. c   5. b
      3. c   6. c
      4. a

4   The woman saw car 3.

---

26 THE TRAIN, BUS & TAXI

1   2. 4:37   5. 5:37 A.M.
      3. 12:07 A.M.   6. 6:37
      4. 10:37

2   2. c   6. c
      3. a   7. a
      4. b   8. c
      5. b

3   2. True
      3. True
      4. False. The off-duty sign is off.
      5. False. The taxi is new and clean.
      6. True

4   2. train   5. track
      3. ticket   6. departure board
      4. counter   7. schedule
      b.

---

27 ROUTES & ROAD SIGNS

1   2. e   7. b
      3. d   8. a
      4. j   9. h
      5. c   10. g
      6. i

2   2. False. There isn't a bus in the picture.
      3. True
      4. True
      5. False. The speed limit is 35.
      6. False. Car number 11 is in the middle lane.
      7. True
      8. False. There isn't a traffic light on the highway.
      9. False. There isn't grass on the divider.
     10. False. There is a broken white line on the highway.

3   The post office is number 5.

---

28 THE AIRPORT

1   2. On Board   6. On Board
      3. Runway   7. Runway
      4. Terminal   8. On Board
      5. Terminal

2   2. luggage carrier   4. tray
      3. cockpit   5. gate

3   2. security check   5. jet
      3. waiting room   6. baggage claim area
      4. gate   7. customs

4   2. security guard   5. pilot/captain
      3. porter/skycap   6. co-pilot
      4. customs officer   7. flight attendant

5   The passenger's boarding pass is number 2.

29 THE WATERFRONT • THE BEACH

1
2. sand (Beach)
3. boardwalk (Beach)
4. dock (Waterfront)
5. umbrella (Beach)
6. lifeguard (Beach)
7. longshoreman (Waterfront)
8. crane (Waterfront)
9. seashell (Beach)
10. ocean (Beach)

2
2. hotel
3. sand castle
4. wave
5. sand
6. rock
7. umbrella
8. tanker

3
2. on
3. in
4. under
5. on
6. on
7. in
8. on

4
2. Waterfront
3. Waterfront
4. Waterfront
5. Beach
6. Beach
7. Waterfront
8. Waterfront

30 WATER SPORTS • WINTER SPORTS

1
2. True
3. False. It's an ice skate.
4. False. It's a helmet.
5. True
6. False. A scuba diver uses it.
7. True
8. False. It's a life jacket.

2
2. Water Sports
3. Water Sports
4. Winter Sports
5. Water Sports
6. Winter Sports
7. Winter Sports
8. Water Sports

3
2. h
3. a
4. b
5. f
6. d
7. j
8. i
9. g
10. c

4
1. b. water skiing
   c. rowing
   d. canoeing
   e. kayaking
   f. white water rafting
2. a. snorkeling
   b. scuba diving
   c. downhill skiing
3. a. kayaking
   b. bobsledding
   c. snowmobiling
4. a. downhill skiing
   b. cross country skiing
5. a. waterskiing
   b. downhill skiing
   c. cross country skiing

5
2. b
3. c
4. c
5. a
6. c

31 SPECTATOR SPORTS • OTHER SPORTS

1
2. f
3. g
4. b
5. e
6. d
7. a
8. h

2 2., 6., 8., 9., 10.

3
2. c
3. b
4. a
5. b
6. c
7. a
8. b
9. c
10. b
11. c
12. c

4

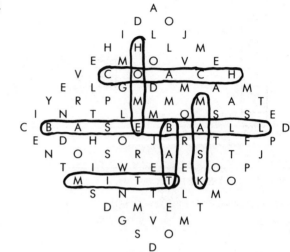

5
2. a
3. b
4. b
5. c
6. b
7. a
8. b
9. c
10. c

32 ENTERTAINMENT • MUSICAL INSTRUMENTS

1
2. flute (Woodwinds)
3. drum (Percussion)
4. guitar (Strings)
5. oboe (Woodwinds)
6. violin (Strings)
7. cello (Strings)
8. cymbal (Percussion)
9. clarinet (Woodwinds)
10. bassoon (Woodwinds)

2 audience, marquee, aisle, orchestra pit

3
2. False. A ballerina/ballet dancer wears toe shoes.
3. True
4. True
5. False. The saxophone is a woodwind instrument.
6. True
7. True
8. True
9. True
10. False. There are footlights on the stage.

4
2. b
3. c
4. c
5. a
6. b
7. c
8. a
9. c
10. c

5

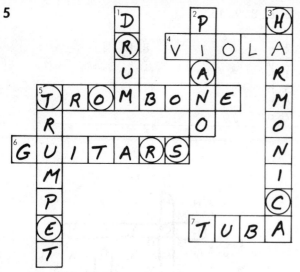

Orchestra

33 THE ZOO & PETS

1 2. whiskers   4. tail
    3. paw   It is a lion.

2 2. a   6. c
    3. h   7. d
    4. b   8. e
    5. g

3 2. camel (Zoo)   6. gorilla (Zoo)
    3. fox (Zoo)   7. goldfish (Home)
    4. parakeet (Home)   8. llama (Zoo)
    5. hamster (Home)   9. hippopotamus (Zoo)

4 2. giraffe   7. turtle
    3. elephant   8. puppy
    4. rhinoceros   9. kitten
    5. frog and kangaroo   10. goldfish
    6. zebra

5 2. leopard   6. kangaroo
    3. horns   7. white
    4. deer   8. cat
    5. turtle

6 2. c   5. a
    3. a   6. c
    4. b   7. a

34 THE FARM • FISH & SEA ANIMALS

1 2. False. There's a pond to the right of the farmhouse.
    3. True
    4. True
    5. False. The tractor is next to the barn.
    6. False. There are three cows on the farm.
    7. True
    8. False. The farmer is on the horse.

2 2. a   4. b
    3. e   5. c

3 2. b   5. a
    3. c   6. b
    4. b   7. b

4 2. Male or Female   7. Male or Female
    3. Female   8. Male or Female
    4. Male or Female   9. Female
    5. Male or Female   10. Male or Female
    6. Male

5 2. b   5. a
    3. c   6. b
    4. b

35 BIRDS • INSECTS & RODENTS

1 2. pelican   6. duck
    3. crane   7. owl
    4. swan   8. pigeon
    5. cockatoo

2 2. bee (Insect)   7. rat (Rodent)
    3. robin (Bird)   8. ostrich (Bird)
    4. squirrel (Rodent)   9. ladybug (Insect)
    5. mosquito (Insect)   10. mouse (Rodent)
    6. eagle (Bird)

3 2. feathers   5. beak
    3. duck   6. nest
    4. pelican
    c

4 2. c   6. c
    3. c   7. c
    4. a   8. b
    5. b

5 2. bat   7. mouse
    3. bill   8. beak
    4. owl   9. tail
    5. duck   10. cricket
    6. fly

36 SPACE • THE MILITARY

1 2. pilot (Air Force)   7. battleship (Navy)
    3. rifle (Army)   8. parachute (Air Force)
    4. bomber (Air Force)   9. jeep (Army)
    5. sailor (Navy)   10. cannon (Army)
    6. submarine (Navy)

2 2. astronaut
    3. parachute
    4. booster rocket

3 2. False. He is an astronaut.
    3. True
    4. True
    5. False. He is wearing a space suit.
    6. False. There is a lunar module/vehicle to the right of the flag.
    7. False. They are soldiers.
    8. True
    9. True

4 2. in   7. in
    3. in   8. on
    4. on   9. on
    5. in   10. on
    6. in

5 2. a   4. c
    3. a   5. b

---

37 HOBBIES & GAMES ●
SEWING & SUNDRIES

1 2. c   5. a
    3. e   6. d
    4. f

2 2. sculpting (Craft)   5. photography (Hobby)
    3. knitting (Craft)   6. checkers (Game)
    4. cards (Game)   7. woodworking (Craft)

3 2. b   6. b
    3. a   7. c
    4. c   8. c
    5. c

4 2. notebook   5. scissors
    3. compass   6. ribbon
    4. masking tape

5 2. b   6. c
    3. a   7. a
    4. b   8. a
    5. a

6

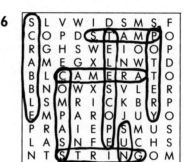